LONGMAN
KEYSTONE

BUILDING BRIDGES

Workbook

Kaye Wiley

PEARSON
Longman

Building Bridges Workbook

Copyright © by Pearson Education, Inc. This program was formerly published as *Shining Star*, Introductory level.

All rights reserved.

No part of this publication may be reproduced, stored in a retrieval system, or transmitted in any form or by any means, electronic, mechanical, photocopying, recording or otherwise, without the prior permission of the publisher.

Pearson Education, 10 Bank Street, White Plains, NY 10606

Staff credits: The people who made up the Longman Keystone Building Bridges team, representing editorial, production, design, manufacturing, and marketing are John Ade, Rhea Banker, Liz Barker, Kenna Bourke, Diane Cipollone, Amanda Rappaport Dobbins, Johnnie Farmer, Warren Fischbach, Patrice Fraccio, Geraldine Geniusas, Charles Green, Aliza Greenblatt, Henry Hild, Ray Keating, Lucille M. Kennedy, Ed Lamprich, Linda Moser, Rebecca Ortman, Liza Pleva, Bill Preston, Edie Pullman, Tania Saiz-Sousa, Chris Siley, Jane Townsend, Lauren Weidenman, and Paula Williams.

Text design: Kirchoff/Wohlberg, Inc.
Text composition: TSI Graphics
Text font: 11/14 Franklin Gothic

Acknowledgment: Paterson Marsh Ltd. "Rain Poem" by Elizabeth Coatsworth. Reprinted by permission of Paterson Marsh Ltd. On behalf of the estate of Elizabeth Coatsworth.

Illustration and photo credits: See page 233.

ISBN-13: 978-0-13-207690-6
ISBN-10: 0-13-207690-X

PEARSON LONGMAN ON THE WEB

Pearsonlongman.com offers online resources for teachers and students. Access our Companion Websites, our online catalog, and our local offices around the world.

Visit us at **pearsonlongman.com**.

Printed in the United States of America
5 6 7 8 9 10—V012—12 11 10

TO THE STUDENT

Welcome to the Workbook for *Longman Keystone Building Bridges*. Exercises in each unit of this workbook will help you practice the skills and strategies you have learned in the *Longman Keystone* program. Fun activities will help you use reading strategies and practice skills in grammar, spelling, vocabulary, writing, proofreading, and editing.

To help you get the most out of your *Longman Keystone* reading experiences, we've added an exciting feature—the Reader's Companion. The Reader's Companion activities at the back of the book will help you better understand the following selections in your Student Book: "Nomads," "Earthquakes," "The Clever Daughter-in-Law," "The Great Minu," "The Blind Men and the Elephant," "Rain Poem," and "Aaron's Gift."

The Reader's Companion begins with a summary. It tells you what the selection is about before you read it. Then a visual summary helps you see the main ideas and the organization of the selection. A Use What You Know question lets you explore your own knowledge and experience before you read. You will use the same reading strategies that you learned in the Student Book. You'll show what you know about the kind of selection you are reading—whether it's a nonfiction text or a poem, for example. Language Link questions test your knowledge of key words or grammar skills taught with that selection. You will also have several chances to check your understanding of each selection. When you see the Mark the Text symbol, you'll know that you should underline, circle, or put a box around the text. You can have fun expressing your creativity as you do the activity at the end of each exercise.

We hope you'll enjoy showing what you know as you complete the many and varied activities included in your *Longman Keystone Building Bridges* Workbook.

CONTENTS

INTRODUCTION Getting Started

Numbers and Letters: Cardinal Numbers 2
Numbers and Letters: Capital and Lowercase Letters 3
Days and Months: Ordinal Numbers 4
Days and Months: Days of the Week and Months of the Year 5
Colors and Shapes 6
Directions: Using Direction Words 8
Classroom Objects: A Picture Dictionary 10
Classroom Objects: My Classroom 11
Reading Strategy: Find Main Idea and Details 12
Reading Strategy: Identify Characters, Plot, and Setting 13
Writing: Understanding the Writing Process 14
Social Studies: Reading Maps 16
Social Studies: Using Timelines 18
Science: Reading about Matter 20
Science: Reading about Ecosystems 22
Mathematics: Using Operations 24
Mathematics: Doing Word Problems 25
Mathematics: Using Fractions 26
Mathematics: Using Fractions, Decimals, and Percents 27
Health and Fitness: Your Body 28
Health and Fitness: Reading about Exercise and Calories 29
Health and Fitness: Reading about Keeping Healthy 30
Health and Fitness: Reading about Healthy and Unhealthy Habits 31

UNIT 1 Journeys

Introduction: Looking Ahead 32
Vocabulary: "Nomads" 33
Word Structure: Singular and Plural Nouns 34
Reading Strategy: Preview 35
Vocabulary Building: Understanding Antonyms 36
Phonics: Review Consonants 37
Phonics: Short *a* and *e* 38
Comprehension: "Nomads" 39
Skills for Writing: Writing Sentences 40
Spelling: Short *a* and *e* 41
Vocabulary: "Jewel in the Sand" 42
Reading Strategy: Draw Conclusions 43
Grammar: Present Tense: Regular Verbs 44
Grammar: Singular and Plural Nouns 45
Comprehension: "Jewel in the Sand" 46
Spelling Patterns: *am, an, ad, en, et, el* 47
Grammar: Articles 48
Vocabulary Building: Understanding Synonyms 49
Skills for Writing: Writing a Journal Entry 50
Writing Practice: Write about "Journeys" 51

UNIT 2 Hidden Forces

Introduction: Looking Ahead 52
Vocabulary: "The Trojan Horse" 53
Extending Vocabulary: Using Key Words 54

CONTENTS

Reading Strategy: Problems and Solutions 55
Vocabulary Building: Understanding Compound Words 56
Phonics: Short *i*, *o*, and *u* 57
Phonics: Review Consonants *c* and *g* 58
Comprehension: "The Trojan Horse" 59
Skills for Writing: Writing Descriptive Sentences 60
Spelling: Short *i*, *o*, and *u* 61
Vocabulary: "Earthquakes" 62
Reading Strategy: Cause and Effect 63
Grammar: Simple Past: Regular Verbs 64
Grammar: Understanding Adjectives 65
Comprehension: "Earthquakes" 66
Spelling Patterns: *in, id, on, ot, un, ud* 67
Grammar: Present and Past Tense: Irregular Verbs 68
Vocabulary Building: Understanding Phrasal Verbs 69
Skills for Writing: Writing a Personal Narrative 70
Writing Practice: Write about "Hidden Forces" 71

UNIT 3 Play Ball!

Introduction: Looking Ahead 72
Vocabulary: "The Bouncing Ball" 73
Extending Vocabulary: Using Key Words 74
Reading Strategy: Ask Questions 75
Vocabulary Building: Understanding the Suffix *-er* 76
Phonics: Long Vowels with Signal *e* 77
Phonics: Review *y* as /y/, Long *e*, and Long *i* 78
Comprehension: "The Bouncing Ball" 79
Skills for Writing: Writing Questions and Answers 80
Spelling: Initial and Final *y* 81
Vocabulary: "Roberto Clemente" 82
Reading Strategy: Understand Chronological Order 83
Grammar: Questions in the Present 84
Grammar: Proper Nouns 85
Comprehension: "Roberto Clemente" 86
Spelling Patterns: Long Vowels with Signal *e* 87
Grammar: Questions 88
Vocabulary Building: Suffix *-ly* 89
Skills for Writing: Biographical Narrative 90
Writing Practice: Write about "Play Ball!" 91

UNIT 4 Family Ties

Introduction: Looking Ahead 92
Vocabulary: "The Clever Daughter-in-Law" 93
Extending Vocabulary: Using Key Words 94
Reading Strategy: Predict 95
Vocabulary Building: Words That Tell *When* 96
Phonics: Initial, Medial, Final Digraphs /ch/, /sh/, /th/ 97
Phonics: *x* /ks/, *qu* /kw/, *wh* /hw/ 98
Comprehension: "The Clever Daughter-in-Law" 99
Skills for Writing: Writing Quotations in Conversations 100
Spelling: Initial, Medial, Final Digraphs *ch*, *sh*, *th* 101

CONTENTS

Vocabulary: "Family Traits" 102
Reading Strategy: Reread 103
Grammar: Single Possessives with Apostrophes 104
Grammar: Plural Possessives 105
Comprehension: "Family Traits" 106
Spelling Patterns: *x, qu, wh* 107
Grammar: Adverbs 108
Vocabulary Building: Homophones 109
Skills for Writing: Writing a Personal Letter 110
Writing Practice: Write about "Family Ties" 111

UNIT 5 The Power of Words

Introduction: Looking Ahead 112
Vocabulary: "Early Writing" 113
Extending Vocabulary: Using Key Words 114
Reading Strategy: Take Notes 115
Vocabulary Building: Collocations 116
Phonics: Long Vowels: *ai, ay, eigh; ee, ea, ei* 117
Phonics: Long Vowels: *oa, oe, ow; ue, ui, ew* 118
Comprehension: "Early Writing" 119
Skills for Writing: Writing Details in Outlines 120
Spelling Patterns: *ai, ay, eigh; ee, ei, ea* 121
Vocabulary: "The Great Minu" 122
Reading Strategy: Understand Irony 123
Grammar: Possessive Pronouns 124
Grammar: Combining Simple Sentences Using *and* 125
Comprehension: "The Great Minu" 126
Spelling Patterns: *oa, oe, ow; ue, ui, ew* 127
Grammar: Pronouns 128
Vocabulary Building: Prefixes *un-, re-* 129
Skills for Writing: Writing Notes for a Report 130
Writing Practice: Write about "The Power of Words" 131

UNIT 6 Exploring the Senses

Introduction: Looking Ahead 132
Vocabulary: "The Blind Men and the Elephant" 133
Extending Vocabulary: Using Key Words 134
Reading Strategy: Make Inferences 135
Vocabulary Building: Ordinal Numbers 136
Phonics: Final *-ed* as /ed/, /d/, /t/; Final *-s* and *-es* as /s/, /z/ 137
Phonics: *r*-controlled Vowels 138
Comprehension: "The Blind Men and the Elephant" 139
Skills for Writing: Poems with Rhyming Words 140
Spelling: Adding *-ing, -ed, -s,* and *-es* to Base Words 141
Vocabulary: "Animal Senses" 142
Reading Strategy: Find Main Ideas 143
Grammar: Prepositions 144
Grammar: Combining Simple Sentences Using *but* 145
Comprehension: "Animal Senses" 146
Spelling Patterns: *ar, er, ir, or, ur* 147
Grammar: Prepositional Phrases 148

CONTENTS

Vocabulary Building: Homographs 149
Skills for Writing: Writing a Descriptive Paragraph 150
Writing Practice: Write about "Exploring the Senses" 151

UNIT 7 The World of Plants
Introduction: Looking Ahead 152
Vocabulary: "Amazing Plants" 153
Extending Vocabulary: Using Key Words 154
Reading Strategy: Use Diagrams 155
Vocabulary Building: Regular Comparatives with *-er* and *-est* 156
Phonics: Final and Medial *tion* 157
Phonics: Diphthongs: *ow, ou; oi, oy; aw, au* 158
Comprehension: "Amazing Plants" 159
Skills for Writing: Writing Similes 160
Spelling: Diphthongs: *ow, ou; oi, oy; aw, au* 161
Vocabulary: "Apollo and Daphne" 162
Reading Strategy: Visualize 163
Grammar: Positive and Negative Sentences 164
Grammar: Sentences with Compound Subjects 165
Comprehension: "Apollo and Daphne" 166
Spelling Patterns: Final *-tion, -sion* 167
Grammar: Comparison with Adjectives 168
Vocabulary Building: Irregular Comparatives 169
Skills for Writing: Writing a Comparison 170
Writing Practice: Write about "Amazing Plants" 171

UNIT 8 Wings
Introduction: Looking Ahead 172
Vocabulary: "Bessie Coleman, American Flyer" 173
Extending Vocabulary: Using Key Words 174
Reading Strategy: Summarize 175
Vocabulary Building: Nouns and Verbs 176
Phonics: One-, Two-, Three-, and Four-Syllable Words; Initial, Medial,
    Final Schwa 177
Phonics: *oo* in *look* and *oo* in *food* 178
Comprehension: "Bessie Coleman, American Flyer" 179
Grammar: Imperatives 180
Skills for Writing: Writing Instructions 181
Spelling: Words with Schwa 182
Vocabulary: "Aaron's Gift" 183
Reading Strategy: Understand an Author's Purpose 184
Grammar: Writing Dates 185
Comprehension: "Aaron's Gift" 186
Grammar: Dialogue 187
Spelling Patterns: Double-Letter Words: *ll, tt, nn, mm, oo* 188
Grammar: Subject-Verb Agreement: Simple Present 189
Vocabulary Building: Same Words in Six Languages 190
Skills for Writing: Writing a Review 191
Writing Practice: Write about "Wings" 192

READER'S COMPANION 193

Name _____ Date _____

INTRODUCTION Getting Started

NUMBERS AND LETTERS

Use with textbook pages 4–5.

Cardinal Numbers
This chart shows some **cardinal** numbers and words.

1 one	11 eleven	21 twenty-one	40 forty
2 two	12 twelve	22 twenty-two	50 fifty
3 three	13 thirteen	23 twenty-three	60 sixty
4 four	14 fourteen	24 twenty-four	70 seventy
5 five	15 fifteen	25 twenty-five	80 eighty
6 six	16 sixteen	26 twenty-six	90 ninety
7 seven	17 seventeen	27 twenty-seven	100 one hundred
8 eight	18 eighteen	28 twenty-eight	1,000 one thousand
9 nine	19 nineteen	29 twenty-nine	500,000 five hundred thousand
10 ten	20 twenty	30 thirty	1,000,000 one million

Underline the number word in each sentence. Then write the cardinal number. Use the chart to help you.

1. Robert is fifteen years old.   _____

2. There are twenty-six letters in the alphabet.   _____

3. A dollar is worth one hundred pennies.   _____

4. Mindy has three brothers.   _____

5. There are twelve months in a year.   _____

Write the word or words for each of these cardinal numbers. Use the chart to help you.

6. 22: _____

7. 70: _____

8. 500,000: _____

9. 11: _____

10. 1,000: _____

11. 49: _____

12. 1,000,000: _____

2   Introduction   Getting Started

Name _____ Date _____

NUMBERS AND LETTERS

Use with textbook pages 4–5.

Capital and Lowercase Letters

This chart shows the letters of the **alphabet**. There is a **capital letter** and a **lowercase letter** for every letter.

Aa	Gg	Mm	Ss	Yy
Bb	Hh	Nn	Tt	Zz
Cc	Ii	Oo	Uu	
Dd	Jj	Pp	Vv	
Ee	Kk	Qq	Ww	
Ff	Ll	Rr	Xx	

Read each capital letter. Write the lowercase letter that is the same letter.

1. A ____   F ____   K ____   P ____

   U ____

   B ____   G ____   L ____   Q ____

   V ____

   C ____   H ____   M ____   R ____

   W ____

Read each capital letter. Write the capital letter that comes next in the alphabet.

2. A ____   I ____   O ____   U ____

   C ____   K ____   Q ____   W ____

   E ____   M ____   S ____   Y ____

   G ____

Introduction   Getting Started

Name _____ Date _____

DAYS AND MONTHS
Use with textbook pages 6–7.

Ordinal Numbers
Ordinal numbers and words are used to show order.

Pablo is the **third** boy in line. Ken is the **sixth** boy in line.

This chart shows some ordinal numbers and words.

1st	first	**11th**	eleventh	**21st**	twenty-first	**40th**	fortieth
2nd	second	**12th**	twelfth	**22nd**	twenty-second	**50th**	fiftieth
3rd	third	**13th**	thirteenth	**23rd**	twenty-third	**60th**	sixtieth
4th	fourth	**14th**	fourteenth	**24th**	twenty-fourth	**70th**	seventieth
5th	fifth	**15th**	fifteenth	**25th**	twenty-fifth	**80th**	eightieth
6th	sixth	**16th**	sixteenth	**26th**	twenty-sixth	**90th**	ninetieth
7th	seventh	**17th**	seventeenth	**27th**	twenty-seventh	**100th**	one hundredth
8th	eighth	**18th**	eighteenth	**28th**	twenty-eighth	**1,000th**	one thousandth
9th	ninth	**19th**	nineteenth	**29th**	twenty-ninth	**500,000th**	five hundred thousandth
10th	tenth	**20th**	twentieth	**30th**	thirtieth	**1,000,000th**	one millionth

Write the ordinal number word or words for each number. Use the words from the chart.

1. 13th _____
2. 18th _____
3. 20th _____
4. 23rd _____
5. 25th _____
6. 28th _____

Underline the ordinal number word in each sentence. Then write the word.

7. January is the first month. _____
8. December is the twelfth month. _____

Name _____   Date _____

DAYS AND MONTHS

Use with textbook pages 6–7.

Days of the Week and Months of the Year
There are seven **days** in a week.

| Monday | Tuesday | Wednesday | Thursday | Friday | Saturday | Sunday |

Underline the word that names a day in each sentence. Then write the word.

1. I read a book on Thursday. _____
2. I played a game on Monday. _____
3. I wrote a letter on Tuesday. _____
4. I found a penny on Friday. _____
5. I saw my friend on Sunday. _____
6. I rode my bike on Wednesday. _____
7. I painted a picture on Saturday. _____

There are twelve **months** in a year.

| January | February | March | April | May | June |
| July | August | September | October | November | December |

Underline the word that names a month in each sentence. Then write the word.

8. I start school in September. _____
9. I play soccer in October. _____
10. I ride my sled in January. _____
11. I fly my kite in March. _____
12. I pick flowers in May. _____
13. I see my grandma in June. _____
14. I draw flags in July. _____

Introduction   Getting Started

Name _____   Date _____

COLORS AND SHAPES

Use with textbook pages 8–9.

Colors

This chart names some **colors**.

red	pink	blue	purple	green	yellow
orange	brown	black	gray	white	tan

Underline two color words in each sentence. Then write the words.

1. Bob has a black and brown hat.　　　_____ _____

2. Pam has a gray and white hat.　　　_____ _____

3. Marco has a blue and green hat.　　_____ _____

4. Cara has a pink and tan hat.　　　 _____ _____

5. Tim has a yellow and red hat.　　　_____ _____

Complete each sentence with a color word from the chart above.

6. Rick painted a _____ house.

7. Luz painted a _____ sky.

8. Ed painted some _____ clouds.

9. Pat painted some _____ birds.

10. Ben painted some _____ flowers.

11. Maria painted some _____ butterflies.

12. Sam painted a _____ bug.

13. Pete painted a _____ cat.

14. Luis painted a _____ dog.

6　　　　　　　　　　　　　　　　**Introduction**　Getting Started

Name _____ Date _____

COLORS AND SHAPES
Use with textbook pages 8–9.

Shapes
These words name some **shapes**.

   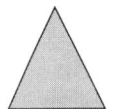 

▲ circle   ▲ square   ▲ rectangle   ▲ triangle   ▲ star

Read each word. Draw the shape.

1. circle   **2.** square   **3.** rectangle   **4.** triangle   **5.** star

Look at each picture. Write the names of the shapes you see. Use the chart to help you.

6. _____ _____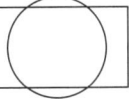

7. _____ _____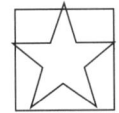

8. _____ _____

9. _____ _____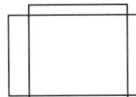

10. _____ _____

Introduction   Getting Started

Name _____ Date _____

DIRECTIONS

Use with textbook pages 10–11.

Using Direction Words

The words below are used to give **directions**.

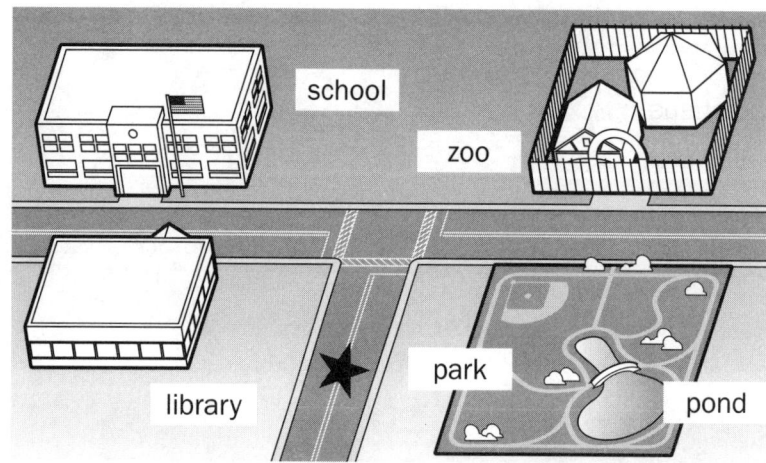

Use the map and follow the directions. Read each question and then circle **Yes** or **No**.

1. Start at the ★. Go to the pond.
   a. Did you go straight and turn left?   Yes   No
   b. Did you go straight and turn right?   Yes   No

2. Start at the ★. Go to the school.
   a. Did you go straight and turn left?   Yes   No
   b. Did you go straight and turn right?   Yes   No

3. Start at the ★. Go to the zoo.
   a. Did you go straight and turn left?   Yes   No
   b. Did you go straight and turn right?   Yes   No

4. Start at the ★. Go to the library.
   a. Did you go straight and turn left?   Yes   No
   b. Did you go straight and turn right?   Yes   No

5. Start at the ★. Go to the park.
   a. Did you go straight and turn left?   Yes   No
   b. Did you go straight and turn right?   Yes   No

Name _____ Date _____

DIRECTIONS

Use with textbook pages 10–11.

Using Direction Words
The words below are also used to give **directions**.

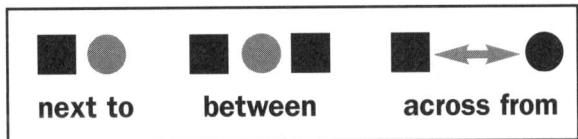

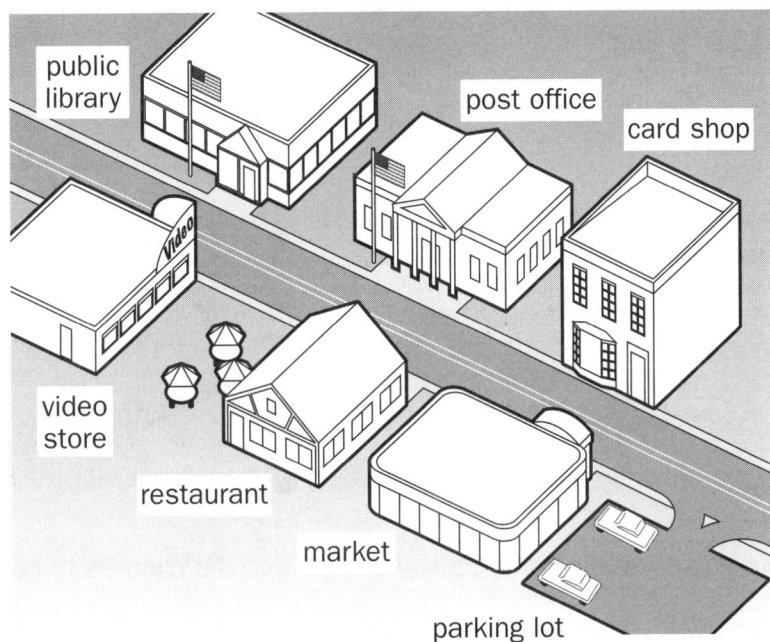

Look at the picture. Complete each sentence with a word or phrase from the box.

> next to   between   across from

1. The library is _____ the video store.

2. The library is _____ the post office.

3. The video store is _____ the restaurant.

4. The restaurant is _____ the video store and the market.

5. The post office is _____ the library and the card shop.

6. The restaurant is _____ the post office.

7. The market is _____ the parking lot.

8. The market is _____ the restaurant and the parking lot.

Introduction   Getting Started   9

Name _____ Date _____

CLASSROOM OBJECTS

Use with textbook pages 12–13.

A Picture Dictionary
Here are some things you may see in your classroom.

▲ clock   ▲ chair   ▲ desk   ▲ globe

▲ book   ▲ map   ▲ pencil   ▲ chalkboard

Write a word to complete each sentence about a classroom. Use the pictures to help you.

1. The teacher writes on the _____ .

2. Each student sits on a _____ .

3. Each student has a _____ to write on.

4. The student writes with a _____ .

5. A _____ shows the world small and round.

6. A _____ shows the world flat and square.

7. There is a _____ on the wall to show the time.

8. The students read a math _____ .

Name _____ Date _____

CLASSROOM OBJECTS

Use with textbook pages 12–13.

My Classroom

1. Draw a picture of your classroom.

2. Describe your classroom using numbers, colors, or directions.

_____
_____
_____
_____
_____
_____
_____

Name _____ Date _____

READING STRATEGY

Use with textbook page 14.

Find Main Idea and Details
When you read nonfiction, find the **main idea** and **details**.

- The **main idea** is the biggest or most important idea.
- **Details** are ideas or facts about the main idea.

Read this social studies text about Antarctica.

Antarctica

The continent of Antarctica is very cold. An ice sheet covers most of the land. The average winter temperature is –60°C (–76°F). Few animals can live there all year. In the summer, animals such as penguins, whales, and seals come to Antarctica to eat food and to breed, or have babies.

Write **MI** on the line if the sentence tells the main idea. Write **D** on the line if the sentence tells a detail.

1. _____ An ice sheet covers most of the land in Antarctica.
2. _____ In the summer, animals such as penguins, whales, and seals come to Antarctica to eat food and to breed, or have babies.
3. _____ The continent of Antarctica is very cold.
4. _____ Few animals can live in Antarctica all year.
5. _____ The average winter temperature in Antarctica is –60°C (–76°F).

6. Write the sentence above that tells the main idea.

_____

_____

12   Introduction   Getting Started

Name _____ Date _____

READING STRATEGY

Use with textbook page 15.

Identify Characters, Plot, and Setting

As you read fiction, think about the **characters**, **plot**, and **setting**.

- The **characters** are the people or animals in the story.
- The **plot** is what happens in the story.
- The **setting** is the time and place of the story.

Read this Native American folktale. Then follow the directions below.

How Bear Lost His Tail

Many years ago in North America, Bear had a long tail.

One cold winter day, Bear saw Fox at the lake. Fox was sitting on the ice next to many fish. "How did you catch those fish?" Bear asked.

"With my tail," Fox lied. He wanted to fool Bear. Bear put his tail into the icy water. Soon Bear was asleep. Fox went home to eat his fish.

When Fox returned, Bear was still sleeping. "Bear!" Fox shouted. "Can you feel a fish on your tail?"

Bear jumped up, and his frozen tail broke off.

And that's why bears have short tails today.

1. Circle the names of the two characters in the story.

2. Write the two names that you circled.

   _____   _____

3. What happened to Bear's tail after he jumped up? Write the answer.

   _____

   _____

4. Underline the sentence that tells the setting.

5. Write the time and the place that you underlined.

   Time: _____

   Place: _____

Introduction   Getting Started   13

Name _____ Date _____

WRITING

Use with textbook pages 16–17.

Understanding the Writing Process

The **writing process** is a series of steps that help you write.

- **Prewrite** Before you can write, you need to brainstorm ideas. When you brainstorm ideas, list them. Then choose the best idea. Make notes about your idea.
- **Draft** A draft is your story or report. Use your notes to write your report or story. Write your ideas in sentences about your topic.
- **Edit** When you edit, you check your writing. You make sure that your sentences are clear and easy to understand. You check your spelling and punctuation.
- **Revise** When you revise your story or report, you add details to make the writing more interesting. You can correct any mistakes, too.
- **Publish** When you publish your writing you share it with the class.

Choose the correct answer for each question and underline it.

1. What is the writing process?

    a. It is a series of steps that help you write.

    b. It is a set of pens and pencils.

2. What can you do with the ideas that you brainstorm?

    a. Write them in a list.

    b. Mail your ideas to a friend.

3. What is a draft?

    a. It is your list of ideas.

    b. It is your story or report.

4. What do you do when you edit your writing?

    a. You write notes.

    b. You check your writing.

5. What do you do when you revise your writing?

    a. You think of an idea.

    b. You add details.

6. What do you do when you publish your writing?

    a. You share it with the class.

    b. You check your spelling.

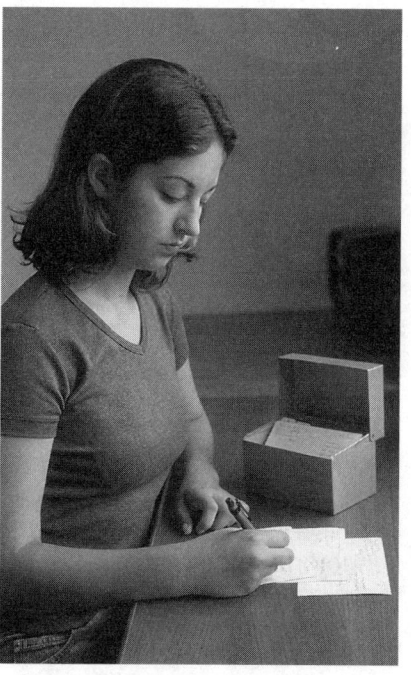

WRITING

Use with textbook pages 16–17.

Understanding the Writing Process

Here are a writer's notes for the story "How Bear Lost His Tail."

Notes for "How Bear Lost His Tail"
Beginning: Bear had a long tail.
Middle: Fox wanted to fool Bear. Fox said he had caught fish with his tail. Bear put his tail into the icy water. Bear fell asleep.
End: Bear's frozen tail broke off.

Choose the correct answer for each question and underline it.

1. What parts did the writer put in her prewriting notes?

    a. She wrote about the beginning, middle, and end.

    b. She wrote only about the end of the story.

2. What is the idea of her story?

    a. The writer wants to tell how Bear lost his tail.

    b. The writer wants to tell why bears sleep in winter.

3. What characters are in the story?

    a. Bear, Pig, and Cat

    b. Bear and Fox

4. What happens at the end of the story?

    a. Bear's frozen tail breaks off.

    b. Bear's tail grows long.

Introduction   Getting Started

Name _____ Date _____

SOCIAL STUDIES
Use with textbook pages 18–19.

Reading Maps
Social studies textbooks often have **maps**. Maps help you understand where people live and where events take place.

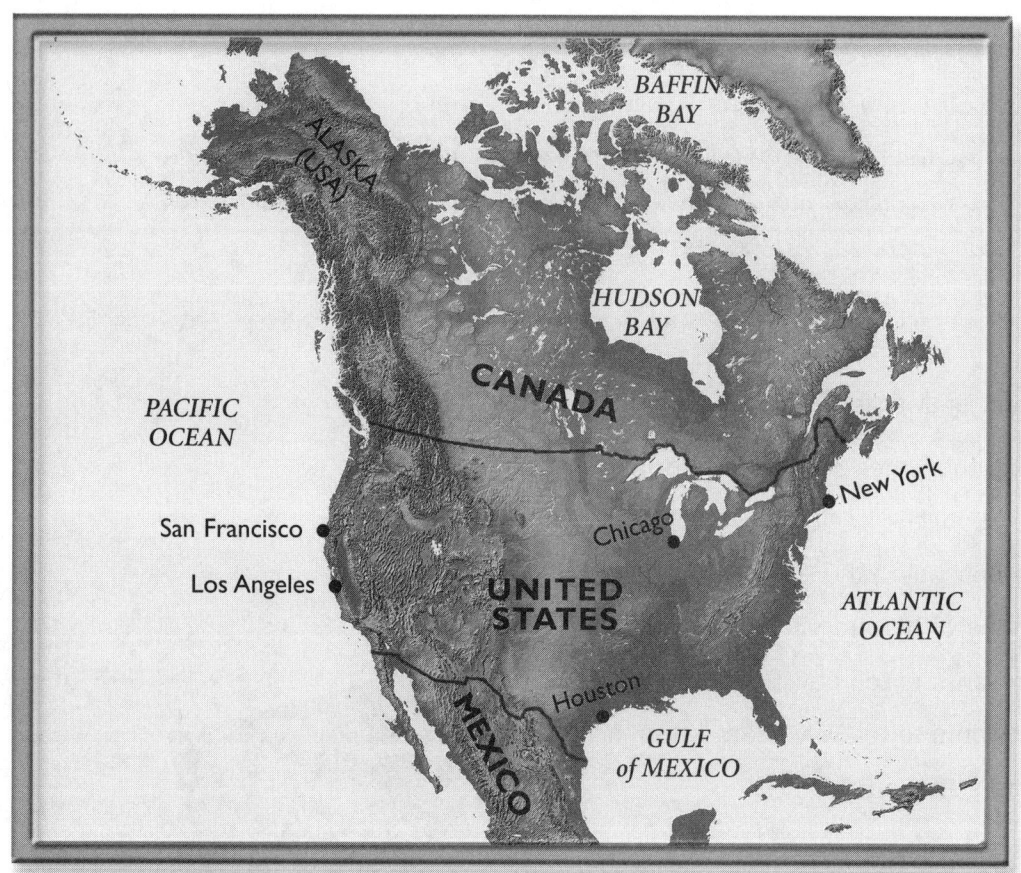

Read each question. Circle the answers.

1. Which three countries are shown on this map?

   a. United States   **b.** Canada   **c.** France   **d.** Mexico

2. Which two oceans are shown on this map?

   a. Indian Ocean   **b.** Atlantic Ocean   **c.** Pacific Ocean

3. Which city is not shown on this map?

   a. New York   **b.** Boston   **c.** Chicago   **d.** Houston

4. Which two bays are shown on this map?

   a. Baffin Bay   **b.** Hudson Bay   **c.** San Francisco Bay

Name _____ Date _____

SOCIAL STUDIES

Use with textbook pages 18–19.

Reading Maps

Maps often have a compass rose. The compass rose shows the directions north (N), south (S), east (E), and west (W). Find the compass rose on this map.

Use the map to answer each question.

1. What country is shown on the map?
   _____

2. What directions are on the compass rose?
   _____   _____

   _____   _____

3. Which state is west of Colorado and begins with the letter *U*? _____

4. Which state is south of Georgia and begins with the letter *F*? _____

5. Which state is east of Minnesota and begins with the letter *W*? _____

6. Which state is north of Tennessee and begins with the letter *K*? _____

Introduction   Getting Started   17

Name _____ Date _____

SOCIAL STUDIES

Use with textbook pages 20–21.

Using Timelines
Timelines help you remember important dates and the order of events in history. This timeline tells about California's history.

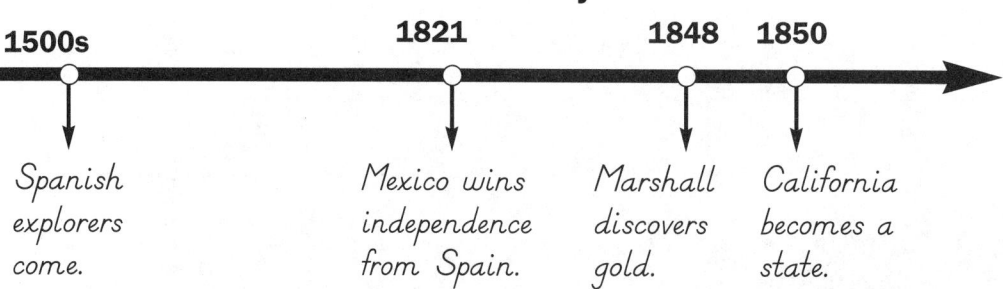

Use the timeline to answer each question.

1. What is the title of the timeline?
   _____

2. In what period does the timeline begin?
   _____

3. What happened in California in the 1500s?
   _____

4. In what year did Mexico win independence from Spain?
   _____

5. What happened in California in 1848?
   _____

6. In what year did California become a state?
   _____

18   Introduction   Getting Started

Name _____   Date _____

SOCIAL STUDIES

Use with textbook pages 20–21.

Using Timelines

Read this text. It tells about part of the history of California. Then follow the directions below.

California, the Golden State

In 1846, Mexico and the United States fought a war. When the peace treaty was signed on February 2, 1848, California became a territory of the United States. Two weeks before, a man named James Marshall discovered something amazing near Sacramento, California. On January 24, 1848, Marshall saw shiny pieces of yellow metal in a stream. They were pieces of gold!

Many people came to California to find gold. They were called "forty-niners" because they came in 1849. Soon people came from all over the world, including China and Australia.

1. What happened in 1846? Add it to the timeline.

2. What happened in 1849? Add it to the timeline.

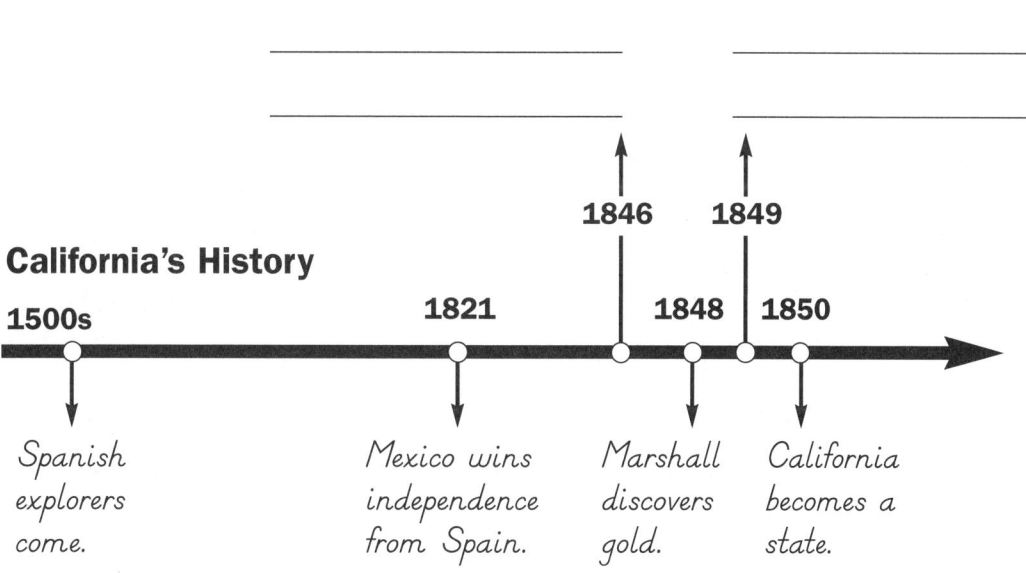

Introduction   Getting Started

Name _____ Date _____

SCIENCE

Use with textbook pages 22–23.

Reading about Matter

Reading science articles helps you learn about the world you live in. Read about the three states of water.

▲ solid   ▲ liquid   ▲ gas

Three States of Water

Water is an important <u>liquid</u>. Water <u>covers</u> about 70 percent of the earth's surface. Your body is about two-thirds <u>water</u>. When water is in its liquid state, you can <u>pour</u> it. As a liquid, water takes the shape of its container. The water in the picture above takes the shape of the glass.

When water gets very cold, it <u>freezes</u>. It <u>changes</u> from a liquid to a solid. The freezing point of water is 0°C (32°F). Ice and <u>snow</u> are solid forms of water.

When water gets very hot, it <u>boils</u>. Then it changes from a liquid to a <u>gas</u>. This gas is called water vapor or <u>steam</u>. The boiling point of water is 100°C (212°F).

Use one of the underlined words in "Three States of Water" to complete each sentence.

1. Water is an important _____ .

2. Water _____ about 70 percent of the earth's surface.

3. Your body is about two-thirds _____ .

4. When water is in its liquid state, you can _____ it.

5. When water gets very cold, it _____ .

6. It _____ from a liquid to a solid.

7. Ice and _____ are solid forms of water.

8. When water gets very hot, it _____ .

9. When water boils, it changes from a liquid to a _____ .

10. This gas is called water vapor or _____ .

Introduction   Getting Started

SCIENCE

Use with textbook pages 22–23.

Reading about Matter
Read about the water cycle.

The Water Cycle

The movement of water from the ground to the air and back is called the water cycle. In the water cycle, water changes its state as it moves. The sun heats water on the ground and changes it to water vapor. This change is called evaporation. Then water vapor moves up in the air and forms clouds. Water vapor cools in the clouds and changes into water drops. This change is called condensation. When the water drops become large enough, they fall from the clouds down to the ground as precipitation, such as rain or snow.

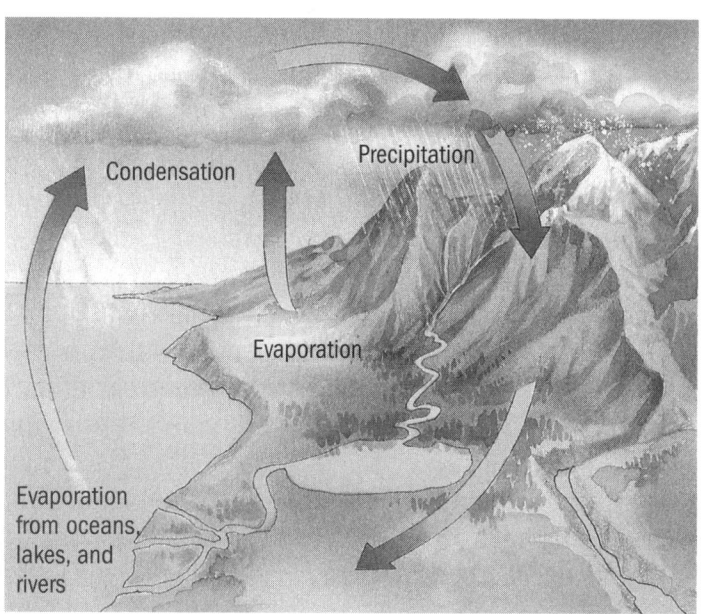

Use one of the underlined words in "The Water Cycle" to complete each sentence.

1. The movement of water from the ground to the air and back is called the

   water _____.

2. In the water cycle, water changes its state as it _____.

3. The _____ heats water on the ground and changes it to water vapor.

4. This _____ is called evaporation.

5. Then water _____ moves up in the air and forms clouds.

6. Water vapor _____ in the clouds and changes into water drops.

7. This change is called _____.

8. When the water drops become large enough, they fall from the clouds down to the

   ground as precipitation, such as _____ or snow.

Introduction   Getting Started

Name _____ Date _____

SCIENCE

Use with textbook pages 24–25.

Reading about Ecosystems
Reading science articles helps you answer questions. Read about ecosystems.

What Is an Ecosystem?
An ecosystem is all the living and nonliving things in an area. Living things include plants and animals.

Producers, Consumers, and Decomposers
There are three kinds of living things in an ecosystem: producers, consumers, and decomposers.

Most plants are producers. They produce, or make, their own food. Animals are consumers. Animals cannot make their own food. They consume, or eat, plants or other animals.

Fungi and bacteria are decomposers. Fungi are like plants, but they live in dark places. Mushrooms are examples of fungi. Bacteria are very tiny things that live in soil, air, and water. Fungi and bacteria decompose, or break down, dead plants and animals. They help the dead plants and animals become part of the soil.

▲ Plants are producers.

▲ Animals are consumers.

▲ Fungi are decomposers.

Choose the correct answer for each question and underline it.

1. What is an ecosystem?

   a. An ecosystem is the way water changes to water vapor.

   b. An ecosystem is all the living and nonliving things in an area.

2. What are the three kinds of living things in an ecosystem?

   a. The three kinds of living things are food, water, and air.

   b. The three kinds of living things are producers, consumers, and decomposers.

3. How do most plants get food?

   a. Most plants make their own food.

   b. Most plants eat animals.

4. How do animals get food?

   a. Animals eat other animals or plants.

   b. Animals make their own food.

22 Introduction Getting Started

SCIENCE

Use with textbook pages 24–25.

Reading about Ecosystems
Read about the food chain.

▲ snake   ▲ grass   ▲ owl   ▲ grasshopper   ▲ toad

What Is a Food Chain?

The way food moves through an ecosystem is called a food chain. A food chain begins with a producer—a plant, such as grass. A small consumer, such as a mouse, eats the grass. Then a larger consumer, such as a hawk, eats the mouse. Decomposers, such as bacteria, break down the hawk when it dies. Its body becomes part of the soil.

Choose the correct answer for each question and underline it.

1. What is a food chain?

   a. The way food moves through an ecosystem.

   b. The way water changes its states.

2. Where does a food chain begin?

   a. It begins with a decomposer.

   b. It begins with a producer.

3. What does this food chain begin with?

   a. This food chain begins with birds.

   b. This food chain begins with grass.

4. What small consumer eats the grass in this food chain?

   a. In this food chain, a mouse eats the grass.

   b. In this food chain, a fish eats the grass.

5. What large consumer eats the mouse in this food chain?

   a. An elephant eats the mouse in this food chain.

   b. A hawk eats the mouse in this food chain.

6. What happens to a hawk when it dies?

   a. The decomposers break down the hawk when it dies.

   b. The producers break down the hawk when it dies.

Introduction   Getting Started

Name _____ Date _____

MATHEMATICS
Use with textbook pages 26–27.

Using Operations
Use **symbols** and **words** to show addition, subtraction, multiplication, and division.

Operations:	addition	subtraction	multiplication	division
Symbols:	+	−	×	÷
Words:	plus	minus	times	divided by

Addition

$\begin{array}{r} 3 \\ +\,4 \\ \hline 7 \end{array}$ or $3 + 4 = 7$ or   Three plus four equals seven.

Subtraction

$\begin{array}{r} 7 \\ -\,4 \\ \hline 3 \end{array}$ or $7 - 4 = 3$ or   Seven minus four equals three.

Multiplication

$\begin{array}{r} 3 \\ \times\,7 \\ \hline 21 \end{array}$ or $3 \times 7 = 21$ or   Three times seven equals twenty-one.

Division

$3\overline{)21}$ (= 7)   or $21 \div 3 = 7$ or   Twenty-one divided by three equals seven.

Write the answer to each problem in words. Then write the problem in numbers.

1. Thirteen plus sixteen equals _____ .   _____

2. Nine times ten equals _____ .   _____

3. Ten divided by five equals _____ .   _____

4. Eighty-two minus twenty-two equals _____ .   _____

5. Forty-seven plus twelve equals _____ .   _____

6. Twenty divided by five equals _____ .   _____

Introduction   Getting Started

Name _____ Date _____

MATHEMATICS

Use with textbook pages 26–27.

Doing Word Problems

A **word problem** is a math problem with words and numbers. You can use addition, subtraction, multiplication, and division to solve word problems.

Steps to Follow When Doing Word Problems
1. Read the word problem carefully.
2. Ask yourself, "What operation do I use to solve the problem?"
3. Look for words in the problem that help you decide which operation to use.
4. Sometimes a picture can help you solve a word problem.

Read each word problem. Follow the steps above and solve each problem.

1. Tim has seventy-five pennies. His mother gives him twenty more. How many does he have in all?

_____

2. Lucia writes two reports every week. How many reports does she write in ten weeks?

_____

3. Eric has thirty-five apples. If he needs seven apples for each pie, how many pies can he bake?

_____

4. Mario has ninety-five stamps in his book. He gives fifty-five stamps to his sister. How many stamps does he have left?

_____

Introduction   Getting Started

Name _____ Date _____

MATHEMATICS

Use with textbook pages 28–29.

Using Fractions

A **fraction** is a number smaller than one.

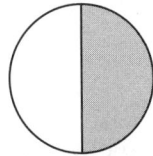 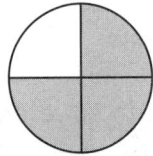 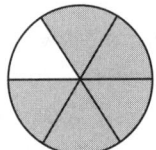

This is 1/2 (one half).   This is 3/4 (three-fourths).   This is 5/6 (five-sixths).

A **fraction** has two numbers divided by a line.

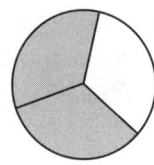 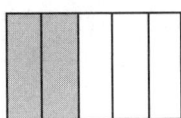 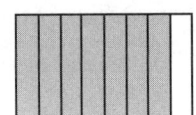

2/3 (two-thirds)   2/5 (two-fifths)   7/8 (seven-eighths)

Write the fraction—numbers and words—for each picture.

1. 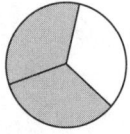 _____ or _____

2.  _____ or _____

3.  _____ or _____

4. 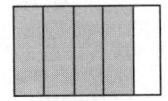 _____ or _____

5.   _____ or _____

6.   _____ or _____

26 Introduction Getting Started

Name _____ Date _____

MATHEMATICS

Use with textbook pages 28–29.

Using Fractions, Decimals, and Percents

A **fraction** is a number smaller than one. A fraction has two numbers divided by a line.

| 1/3 | 3/4 | 5/8 |

A **decimal** is a number smaller than one. A decimal has a decimal point (.) and a number.

| .4 | .25 | .7 |

A **percent** is a part of 100. A percent has a number and a percent symbol (%).

| 5% | 45% | 80% |

Fractions, decimals, and percents can show the same amount or part of something.

Fraction: 1/5 of the circle is shaded. [1/5 = 1 divided by 5]

Decimal: .20 of the circle is shaded. [1/5 = 20/100 = .20]

Percent: 20% of the circle is shaded. [.20 × 100 = 20%]

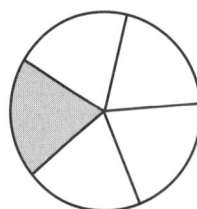

Look at each picture. Complete the answer to show the same amount as a fraction, a decimal, and a percent.

1. Fraction: _____ of the circle is shaded.

   Decimal: .80 of the circle is shaded.

   Percent: 80% of the circle is shaded.

   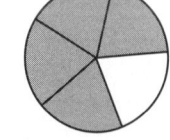

2. Fraction: 2/5 of the circle is shaded.

   Decimal: .40 of the circle is shaded.

   Percent: _____ of the circle is shaded.

   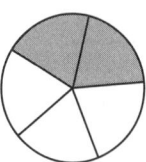

3. Fraction: 3/5 of the circle is shaded.

   Decimal: _____ of the circle is shaded.

   Percent: 60% of the circle is shaded.

   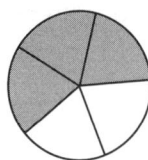

Introduction   Getting Started

Name _____ Date _____

HEALTH AND FITNESS
Use with textbook pages 30–31.

Reading about Your Body
Diagrams help you understand and remember important information. Many diagrams use pictures with labels, or words. This diagram shows different body parts.

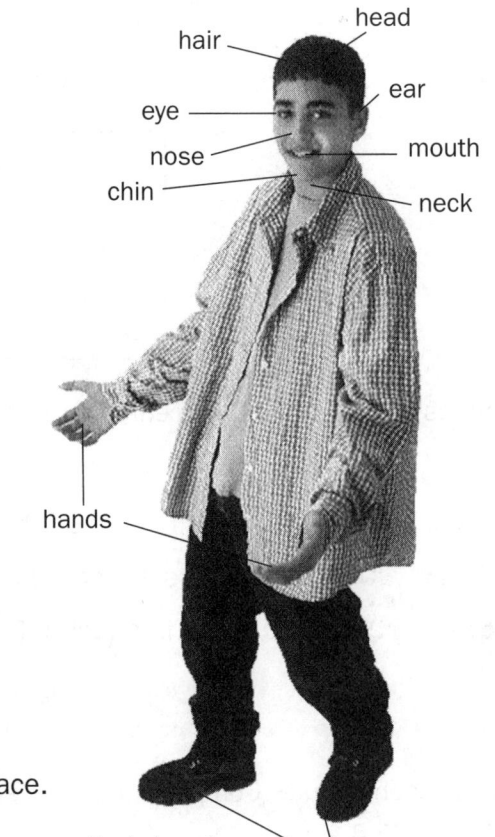

| nose | mouth | hair |
| eyes | chin | ears |

Complete each sentence with a word from the box.

1. We see with our _____.

2. We use our _____ to hear.

3. We eat food with our _____.

4. A _____ is used for smelling.

5. A _____ is at the bottom of a face.

6. Most babies have very little _____ on their heads.

| head | neck | feet | hands |

Answer each question with a word from the box.

7. On what part of the body do you wear gloves? _____

8. On what part of the body do you wear shoes? _____

9. On what part of the body do you wear a hat? _____

10. On what part of the body do you wear a scarf? _____

Name _____ Date _____

HEALTH AND FITNESS

Use with textbook pages 30–31.

Reading about Exercise and Calories
Reading articles helps you answer questions about good health. Read about why exercise is important. Then follow the directions below.

Why Is Exercise Important?
Physical exercise is good for your body. It helps your bones and muscles stay strong. Some people like aerobic exercise. Others enjoy sports such as golf or tennis.

A calorie is a unit for measuring how much energy your body gets from food. Exercise burns, or uses, calories to keep your body healthy and strong.

1. Underline the sentence that tells what exercise does for bones and muscles.

2. Underline the sentence that tells what a calorie is.

Bar graphs are used to compare information. This bar graph shows how many calories each activity burns.

Exercise and Calories

Activity	Calories Burned in One Hour
Golf	~220
Dancing	~270
Tennis	~320
Aerobics	~470
Swimming	~520
Running	~710

Read the bar graph. Answer each question.

3. Which activity uses about 300 calories in one hour? _____

4. Which activity uses about 450 calories in one hour? _____

5. Which activity uses more calories, tennis or golf? _____

6. To burn the most calories, which activity would you do? _____

7. Which activity would you like to do on a warm spring day? _____

Introduction   Getting Started

Name _____ Date _____

HEALTH AND FITNESS

Use with textbook pages 32–33.

Reading about Keeping Healthy
This diagram shows the Food Pyramid.

The Food Pyramid
To keep healthy, eat more foods from the bottom of the pyramid. Foods from the top, such as candy and cake, have a lot of fat and sugar. Eat less of these foods.

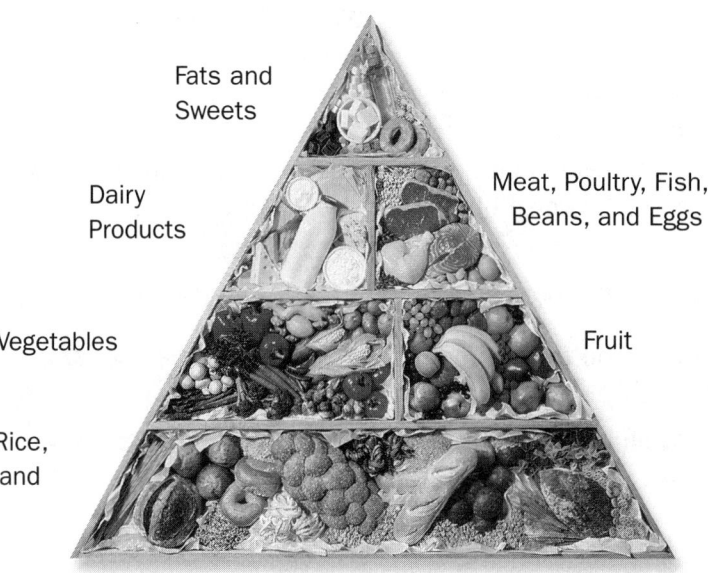

Read each sentence. Write *True* or *Not True*. Use the diagram to help you.

1. Meat is in the same food group as fish. _____
2. Poultry and vegetables are in the same group. _____
3. Bread is in the same group as fruit. _____
4. Beans and eggs are in the same group. _____
5. Eggs are in the same group as rice. _____
6. Rice is in the same group as bread, cereal, and pasta. _____
7. Fats are in the same group as dairy products. _____
8. Fats and sweets are in the same group. _____
9. You should eat less fats and sweets than vegetables. _____
10. You should eat more meat than fruit. _____

Name _____   Date _____

HEALTH AND FITNESS

Use with textbook pages 32–33.

Reading about Healthy and Unhealthy Habits
Read about healthy and unhealthy habits. Then follow the directions below.

What Are Healthy and Unhealthy Habits?
A habit is something you do often or every day. Exercise and eating healthy food are two examples of good, or healthy, habits. Smoking and eating a lot of sweet and fatty foods are examples of bad, or unhealthy, habits.

1. Underline the sentence that tells what a habit is.
2. Underline the sentence that shows examples of good, or healthy, habits.

Read each example and decide whether it is a healthy or unhealthy habit. Write *Healthy Habit* or *Unhealthy Habit* next to each example.

3. doing exercise in a gym   _____
4. eating lots of candy   _____
5. drinking milk   _____
6. drinking water   _____
7. sleeping four hours a night   _____
8. walking or running for exercise   _____
9. eating lots of fatty chips   _____
10. getting a check-up at the doctor _____
11. eating lots of vegetables   _____
12. eating lots of fruits   _____
13. smoking   _____
14. brushing and flossing your teeth _____
15. wearing warm clothes when it is cold _____

Introduction   Getting Started

Name _____ Date _____

UNIT 1 Journeys

INTRODUCTION: LOOKING AHEAD

Use with textbook pages 34–36.

Complete each sentence with a word from the box. Use printing and cursive writing.

desert	camels	nomads	jewel
desert	*camels*	*nomads*	*jewel*

1. I see camels.

   I will learn about _____.

   I will learn about _____.

2. I see a desert.

   I will learn about living in a _____.

   I will learn about living in a _____.

3. I see nomads leading camels.

   I will learn about the life of _____.

   I will learn about the life of _____.

4. I see a beautiful jewel.

   I will read a story about a _____.

   I will read a story about a _____.

Here are the titles of the selections you will read. Complete each sentence with the correct title.

"Jewel in the Sand"   "Nomads"

5. The title of the nonfiction selection I will read is _____.

6. The title of the folktale I will read is _____.

Unit 1 Journeys

Name _____ Date _____

VOCABULARY

Use with textbook page 37.

"Nomads"

Key Words
buffalo   camels   desert   herds   nomads   tents

▲ a herd of buffalo   ▲ tents in a desert   ▲ nomads and camels

Circle the Key Word in each sentence.

1. Buffalo are animals that live on the plains.
2. Herds are groups of animals that live together.
3. Nomads move from place to place.
4. Camels are animals that live in the desert.
5. A desert is a very dry place.
6. Tents are homes that can be moved from place to place.

Write each sentence that is true.

Buffalo travel in herds.
Herds are groups of plants.

7. _____

Nomads move from place to place.
Nomads stay in one place.

8. _____

It is very wet in a desert.
It is very dry in a desert.

9. _____

Unit 1   Journeys   33

Name _____ Date _____

WORD STRUCTURE
Use after the grammar lesson.

Singular and Plural Nouns
Most words have -s added to show more than one. Some words don't have -s added.

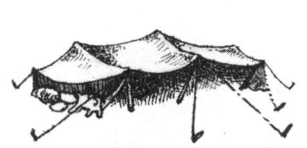   

▲ a tent   ▲ two tents   ▲ one sheep   ▲ two sheep

One	More Than One
camel	camels
herd	herds
sheik	sheiks
nomad	nomads
desert	deserts
tent	tents
buffalo	buffalo
sheep	sheep

Choose a word and use it to complete each sentence.

1. A (desert / deserts) _____ is a very dry place.
2. There are many dry (desert / deserts) _____ in the world.
3. Large (herd / herds) _____ of buffalo race across the plains.
4. Sometimes (camel / camels) _____ follow each other in a line.
5. People called (nomad / nomads) _____ move from place to place.
6. Nomads sleep in (tent / tents) _____ .
7. Some nomads keep a (herd / herds) _____ of sheep.
8. A (nomad / nomads) _____ takes all of his things when he moves.
9. Sometimes a nomad leader is called a (sheik / sheiks) _____ .
10. A (camel / camels) _____ can go many days without food or water.

Name _____ Date _____

READING STRATEGY

Use with textbook page 37.

Preview

Preview means to look at the pages before you read. Follow these steps when you preview the text on pages 38–41:

- Look at the headings in dark type.
- Look at the pictures and maps.
- Try to guess what the text is about.

Look at the text on page 38 in your book.

1. Write the title. It is in big dark type.

   Title: _____

2. Write the two headings that are in smaller dark type.

   _____

   _____

Look at the text and the map on page 39 in your book.

3. Write the two headings.

   _____

   _____

4. Write the names of two places shown on the map.

   _____   _____

Look at the pictures on pages 40 and 41 in your book.

5. Circle the words that tell what you see.

horses	tents	building
bicycle	buffalo	hunters
telephone	desert	boat
car	train	camels

Unit 1   Journeys   35

Name _____ Date _____

VOCABULARY BUILDING

Use after the vocabulary lesson.

Understanding Antonyms

Antonyms are words that mean the opposite of each other.

▲ a few insects   ▲ many insects   ▲ a small tree   ▲ a large tree

Read each sentence and find the underlined word. Write the underlined word and then write its antonym. Use the chart to help you.

good	bad	few	many	north	south
far	near	large	small	protect	hurt
often	seldom	find	lose	famous	unknown
young	old				

1. There are <u>few</u> nomads in North America. _____ _____

2. Camels are <u>good</u> desert animals. _____ _____

3. Yurts <u>protect</u> the nomads who live in them. _____ _____

4. Canada is <u>north</u> of the United States. _____ _____

5. Nomads live <u>far</u> from cities. _____ _____

6. <u>Young</u> Mongolian children learn to race horses. _____ _____

7. Mongolian nomads are <u>famous</u> for horseback riding. _____ _____

8. Nomads move to <u>find</u> food. _____ _____

9. Nomads <u>often</u> live in tents. _____ _____

10. Nomads travel in <u>large</u> family groups. _____ _____

Name _____ Date _____

PHONICS
Use after the phonics lesson.

Review Consonants
Say the beginning sound for each picture.

/b/ boat	/d/ duck	/f/ fish	/h/ horse	/j/ jet
/k/ kite	/l/ lion	/m/ mitten	/n/ nine	/p/ pig
/r/ ring	/s/ sun	/t/ ten	/v/ vase	/w/ wagon	/z/ zebra

Next to each letter, write a word that begins with that letter. Use the words in the box.

nomads	kayaks	villages	seals
tents	meat	far	jump
homes	desert	live	rugs
women	boats	people	zoom

1. b _____
2. j _____
3. n _____
4. t _____

5. d _____
6. k _____
7. p _____
8. v _____

9. f _____
10. l _____
11. r _____
12. w _____

13. h _____
14. m _____
15. s _____
16. z _____

Unit 1   Journeys

Name _____   Date _____

PHONICS

Use after the phonics lesson.

Short *a* and *e*

The letters *a* and *e* often stand for short vowel sounds.

Short *a* is the middle sound you hear in the word *map*. Short *a* is the first sound you hear in the word *Africa*. Short *e* is the middle sound you hear in the word *tent*.

▲ This is a map of Africa.

▲ This is a Bedouin tent.

Read the words for each vowel sound in the chart. Write a rhyming word next to each word.

Short *a*	Short *e*
1. man _____	5. get _____
2. hat _____	6. ten _____
3. dad _____	7. red _____
4. map _____	8. leg _____

Read the words in the box below. Use the words to answer the riddles.

| cap   pan   red   pet |

9. I have the same vowel sound as *map*.
I rhyme with *man*.
I am used for frying things.
What am I?

I am a _____.

10. I have the same vowel sound as *tent*.
I rhyme with *jet*.
People keep me in their homes.
What am I?

I am a _____.

11. I have the same vowel sound as *map*.
I rhyme with *tap*.
You can wear me on your head.
What am I?

I am a _____.

12. I have the same vowel sound as *tent*.
I rhyme with *fed*.
I am a color.
What am I?

I am _____.

Name _____ Date _____

COMPREHENSION

Use with textbook page 42.

"Nomads"
Write a word from the box to complete each sentence in the paragraphs about nomads.

| cities | buffalo | camels | seals | water |
| deserts | plains | move | yurts | sea |

Nomads are people who _____1._____ from place to place. They need to find food and _____2._____ . They live far from most _____3._____ . Some nomads live in dry _____4._____ . Others live on grassy _____5._____ .

In the past, Inuit nomads lived by the _____6._____ in summer. In winter, the Inuit nomads hunted polar bears and _____7._____ . Sioux hunters hunted _____8._____ on the plains of North America.

Today Mongolian nomads live in homes called _____9._____ . Bedouins are nomads who use _____10._____ to carry their goods.

Write the paragraph that tells about two nomad groups of the past. Use cursive writing.

_____
_____
_____
_____

Unit 1   Journeys   39

Name _____ Date _____

SKILLS FOR WRITING

Writing Sentences

A sentence begins with a **capital letter**. A sentence usually ends with a **period**.

      This book is about life in a desert**.**

A sentence that asks a question ends with a **question mark**.

      Do Bedouins keep sheep**?**

Write each group of words as a sentence. Begin with a capital letter and end with a period.

1. some nomads live in deserts
   _____

2. camels carry people and their things
   _____

3. many clans make a tribe
   _____

Write each group of words as a sentence. Begin with a capital letter and end with a question mark.

4. why do nomads move so often
   _____

5. what is a kayak
   _____

6. who learns to ride horses
   _____

Name _____ Date _____

SPELLING

Use after the spelling lesson.

Spelling Short *a* and *e*
Some words with short *a* and short *e* have the **consonant-vowel-consonant** (C-V-C) spelling pattern.

C-V-C	C-V-C
s-a-d	m-e-n
sad	*men*

Circle the word in each sentence that follows the C-V-C spelling pattern. Print the word. Then write the word in cursive.

1. Nomads can travel across a desert. _____ _____
2. They ride on camels that have tan coats. _____ _____
3. Mongolian men ride on horses. _____ _____
4. Sometimes the desert weather is bad. _____ _____
5. Nomads set up tents in the desert sand. _____ _____
6. Bedouins get food for their camels. _____ _____

Write two words from the box to answer each question.

pet	men	tan	net
fan	hat	mat	hen

7. Which two words rhyme with *cat*? _____ and _____
8. Which two words rhyme with *get*? _____ and _____
9. Which two words rhyme with *pen*? _____ and _____
10. Which two words rhyme with *man*? _____ and _____

Write two rhyming pairs in cursive.

11. _____ _____
12. _____ _____

Name _____ Date _____

VOCABULARY

Use with textbook page 45.

"Jewel in the Sand"

Key Words			
daughter	earrings	jewels	nephew
princess	uncle	welcomed	

Circle the Key Word in each sentence.

1. A princess is a girl child of a king or a prince.
2. Your nephew is the son of your brother or sister.
3. Jewels are precious stones.
4. A daughter is someone's female child.
5. *Welcomed* means greeted in a friendly way.
6. Earrings are worn on a person's ears.
7. Your uncle is your mother's brother or your father's brother.

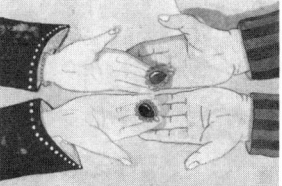
▲ a pair of earrings

▲ an uncle and his nephew

Write each sentence that is true.

A daughter is the sister of a father.
A daughter is the female child of a father.

8. _____

Her uncle is her mother's brother.
Her uncle is her mother's sister.

9. _____

A princess is the son of a prince.
A princess is the daughter of a prince.

10. _____

Two earrings are a pair.
One earring is a pair.

11. _____

Name _____ Date _____

READING STRATEGY

Use with textbook page 45.

Draw Conclusions

To **draw a conclusion** means to decide something is true based on information. For example, if you see someone riding fast on a horse, you might draw the conclusion that the person is a good rider.

- As you read, think about how characters act.
- Based on their actions, draw conclusions about characters.

Read these sentences from the story "Jewel in the Sand."

   Sheik Hamid and his nephew Ali were riding their horses across the desert. The sheik was telling a long story. Suddenly, Ali saw something bright in the sand. Was it a jewel? He was curious, but he did not stop. It was not polite to interrupt his uncle's story.
   Soon the two riders arrived at their camp. Friends welcomed them.

Write each sentence that is a conclusion that you can draw from your reading.

   Ali knew that jewels may be bright.
   Ali had never seen a jewel.

1. _____

   Ali was a polite young man.
   Ali was never polite.

2. _____

   Their friends were sad to see them.
   Their friends were glad to see them.

3. _____

Unit 1   Journeys   43

Name _____   Date _____

GRAMMAR

Use after the grammar lesson.

Present Tense: Regular Verbs

A **verb** shows an action or a state of being. Some verbs are **regular verbs**. For regular verbs, use the base form of the verb with *I, you, we,* and *they*. Add *-s* or *-es* to the base form of the verb with *he, she,* or *it*.

I look.	We look.	I wish.	We wish.
You look.	You look.	You wish.	You wish.
He look**s**.	They look.	He wish**es**.	They wish.
She look**s**.		She wish**es**.	
It look**s**.		It wish**es**.	

Underline the present-tense form of the verb in each sentence.

1. I find beautiful stones with my friend.
2. We pick up some colorful stones.
3. They glow in the sunlight.
4. I show the stones to my mother.
5. She washes them for me.

Complete each sentence with the present-tense form of the verb in parentheses.

6. I (enter) _____ a very long black tent.
7. I (look) _____ at a beautiful princess.
8. She (ask) _____ me to stay.
9. We (talk) _____ for a while.
10. I (show) _____ her one earring.
11. She (show) _____ me the matching earring.
12. She (hand) _____ me the pair of earrings.
13. Sheik Hamid (travel) _____ to meet this princess.
14. He (wish) _____ to be her husband.
15. He (speak) _____ with the princess's father.

Name _____ Date _____

GRAMMAR

Use after the grammar lesson.

Singular and Plural Nouns
Singular nouns name one person, place, or thing.

> princess   desert   earring

Plural nouns name more than one person, place, or thing. Add -s or -es to the noun to form the plural.

> princess**es**   desert**s**   earring**s**

Underline each singular noun in the sentences below.

1. A man traveled in the desert.
2. He traveled day and night.
3. His horse ran very fast.
4. The hot sun was very strong.
5. Each morning was very hot.
6. Each evening was very cool.
7. This tired traveler wanted to get to his home.
8. He wanted to see his uncle.
9. He wanted to rest in a comfortable tent.
10. He wanted a good meal.

Complete each sentence with the plural form of the noun in parentheses.

11. A king made (plan) _____ for a wedding.
12. The king gave many (gift) _____ to his daughter.
13. He gave her four beautiful (horse) _____ .
14. He gave her two bright red (jewel) _____ .
15. He gave her several pretty (dress) _____ .
16. Many (guest) _____ came to the wedding.
17. The wedding celebrations lasted for three (day) _____ .
18. The guests came from faraway (place) _____ .
19. They enjoyed several huge (feast) _____ .
20. The guests gave all their good (wish) _____ .

Unit 1   Journeys

Name _____ Date _____

COMPREHENSION

Use with textbook page 50.

"Jewel in the Sand"
Write a word from the box to complete each sentence about "Jewel in the Sand."

| jewel | princess | nephew | sword |
| uncle | earring | camp | wedding |

Sheik Hamid was traveling with his _____ Ali. Suddenly Ali saw
                                      1.
something bright in the sand. He did not stop. Ali dragged his _____
                                                                        2.
in the sand to leave a trail. Ali returned to his _____. Later he followed
                                                        3.
the trail back and found the _____. Ali showed the jewel to his
                                    4.
_____.
      5.
Sheik Hamid asked an old woman to find the _____ who lost the
                                                      6.
jewel. The princess was happy to see her missing jewel. She took out a matching

_____. Then the kind princess gave the woman the pair of earrings.
      7.
Sheik Hamid traveled to the princess's camp. He wanted to marry her. On the day of

the _____, a young man said he loved the princess. Sheik Hamid said
          8.
the young man could marry the princess. She and the young man were so happy.

Write the last two sentences of the story. Use cursive writing.

_____

_____

_____

_____

_____

46 Unit 1 Journeys

Name _____ Date _____

SPELLING PATTERNS

Use after the spelling lesson.

am, an, ad, en, et, el

Complete each word with the spelling patterns *am, en, an, et, ad,* and *el*.

am	an	ad
c ___ ___ el	h ___ ___ d	h ___ ___
f ___ ___ ilies	___ ___ imals	gl ___ ___
st ___ ___ p	cl ___ ___ s	nom ___ ___ s
en	**et**	**el**
___ ___ ter	g ___ ___	h ___ ___ p
s ___ ___ d	l ___ ___	___ ___ ephant
g ___ ___ erous	blank ___ ___	w ___ ___ comed

Read each sentence. Find the correct word from the chart and fill in the missing letters.

1. Write the word that is the name of an animal.   ___ am ___ ___

2. Write the word that means *more than one family*.   ___ am ___ ___ ___ ___ ___

3. Write the word that begins with *h* and ends with *d*.   ___ an ___

4. Write the word that means *more than one clan*.   ___ ___ an ___

5. Write the word that names people who travel from place to place.   ___ ___ ___ ad ___

6. Write the word that begins with the letters *gl*.   ___ ___ ad

7. Write the word that means *to go in*.   en ___ ___ ___

8. Write the word that ends with the letters *ous*.   ___ en ___ ___ ___ ___ ___

9. Write the word that begins with the letters *bl*.   ___ ___ ___ ___ ___ et

10. Write the two words that rhyme.   ___ et   ___ et

11. Write the word that names an animal with a trunk.   el ___ ___ ___ ___ ___

12. Write the word that means *greeted*.   ___ el ___ ___ ___ ___ ___

Unit 1   Journeys

Name _____ Date _____

GRAMMAR

Use with textbook page 52.

Articles

Articles are small words that identify nouns. *The* and *a* are articles.

    the nomads   **a** group

The word *the* is a **definite article**. It identifies a specific noun. The word *the* is the same for singular and plural nouns.

    the camel   **the** camels

The words *a* and *some* are **indefinite articles**. They identify general nouns. The word *a* is used for singular nouns. *Some* is used for plural nouns.

    a tent   **some** tents

The word *an* is used in place of *a* before a singular noun that begins with a vowel.

    an animal

You don't need an article before the following nouns:

- Names of places, months, days, or languages: **California**, **June**, **Friday**, **Spanish**
- General plurals: They ride **horses**.
- Nouns that can't be counted: There was **ice** on the lake.

Underline the article, or articles, in each sentence.

1. I walked near a beautiful yurt.
2. It was a big, round tent.
3. I met a friend standing there.
4. I saw some children playing by the tent.
5. The children were very busy.
6. Some children were feeding an animal.
7. It was a baby goat.
8. The baby goat drank some milk.

Write *the*, *some*, *a,* or *an* before each noun in the questions below.

9. What is _____ yurt?
10. What did _____ man do?
11. What were _____ children doing?
12. Who fed _____ animal?

48   **Unit 1** Journeys

Name _____ Date _____

VOCABULARY BUILDING

Use after the vocabulary lesson.

Understanding Synonyms

Synonyms are words that have the same or nearly the same meaning. Read the pairs of synonyms in the chart below.

right	correct
curious	interested
sparkling	shining
idea	thought
later	afterward
welcomed	greeted
beautiful	pretty
fear	fright
guest	visitor
joy	happiness

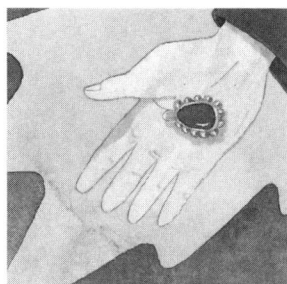

▲ a **pretty** earring; a **beautiful** earring

Read each sentence and find the underlined word. Write the underlined word and then write its synonym. Use the chart to help you.

1. Ali saw a jewel sparkling in the sand.   _____ _____

2. The jewel was beautiful.   _____ _____

3. Ali was curious about the jewel.   _____ _____

4. Ali had an idea.   _____ _____

5. Later Ali would return to look for the jewel.   _____ _____

6. Friends welcomed the men to the camp.   _____ _____

7. Sheik Hamid was the guest of the princess's father.   _____ _____

8. The young man spoke to Sheik Hamid without fear.   _____ _____

9. Sheik Hamid hoped the princess would find joy.   _____ _____

10. Sheik Hamid did what was right.   _____ _____

Unit 1   Journeys

Name _____ Date _____

SKILLS FOR WRITING
Use with textbook page 53.

Writing a Journal Entry

People write in journals to record their thoughts and feelings about things that happen in their lives. Each separate writing in a journal is called a **journal entry**. A journal entry is personal and informal.

Read this journal entry.

> *September 29*
>
> Today was wonderful. I thought it was going to be a hard day at school for me. I was having my first spelling test of the year. But it turned out to be a great day. I had really studied the word list. I spelled every word on the test correctly. My score was 100%.
>
> In the afternoon I played baseball. I hit the first ball that was pitched to me. I thought it was going to be a fly ball. I ran as fast as I could. No one caught the ball. I scored a home run. Everyone cheered and I felt really happy. It really was a great day. I wonder what kind of day tomorrow will be.

Circle the answer to each question.

1. What school happening does this journal entry describe?

    a. a math test **b.** a science class **c.** a spelling test

2. What after-school activity does this journal entry describe?

    a. a baseball game **b.** a soccer game **c.** a kite contest

3. What personal information do you learn about the boy?

    a. his eye color **b.** his spelling score **c.** his age

Write an answer to each question.

4. How do you think the writer was feeling when he wrote this entry?

   _____

5. What do you learn about the writer from reading his journal entry?

   _____

Name _____   Date _____

WRITING PRACTICE

Write about "Journeys"
Think about what you read about in Unit 1.

What did you learn about nomads? Why do they move their homes so much? What are their lives like? Write three sentences about nomads. Here are some words you might want to use.

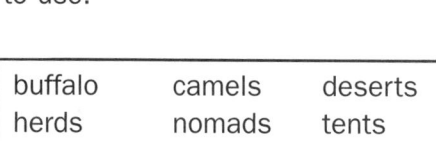

| buffalo | camels | deserts |
| herds | nomads | tents |

_____
_____
_____
_____
_____

What was so special about the jewel the nephew found in the sand? Why is the ending of the story a happy one? What does it show you? Write three sentences about your thoughts on this story.

_____
_____
_____
_____
_____

Unit 1   Journeys

Name _____ Date _____

UNIT 2 Hidden Forces

INTRODUCTION: LOOKING AHEAD

Use with textbook pages 56–58.

Complete each sentence with a word from the box. Use printing and cursive writing.

palace	building	horse
palace	*building*	*horse*

1. I see a palace.

   I will find out who lives in a _____.

   I will find out who lives in a _____.

2. I see a wooden horse.

   I will find out who built a wooden _____.

   I will find out who built a wooden _____.

3. I see a building that has fallen down.

   I will find out why the _____ fell.

   I will find out why the _____ fell.

Here are the titles of the selections you will read. Complete each sentence with the correct title.

"The Trojan Horse"   "Earthquakes"

4. The title of the nonfiction selection I will read is _____.

5. The title of the legend I will read is _____.

52 Unit 2 Hidden Forces

Name _____ Date _____

VOCABULARY

Use with textbook page 59.

"The Trojan Horse"

Key Words		
attack	enemies	palace
prisoner	soldiers	strong

▲ a beautiful palace

▲ soldiers fighting the enemies

▲ strong high walls

Circle the Key Word in each sentence.

1. A palace is the home of a king, queen, prince, or princess.
2. Soldiers are members of an army.
3. A prisoner is not a free person.
4. Something that is strong is hard to break down.
5. To attack means to strike with force.
6. Enemies are people who fight each other.

Write each sentence that is true.

A strong wall is hard to bring down.
A strong wall falls apart easily.

7. _____

A king usually lives in a palace.
A king usually lives in a barn.

8. _____

Horses are beautiful birds.
Horses are beautiful animals.

9. _____

Unit 2 Hidden Forces   53

Name _____ Date _____

EXTENDING VOCABULARY

Use with textbook page 59.

Using Key Words

Read each Key Word. Then read the words that mean almost the same as the Key Word.

Key Word	Words That Mean Almost the Same
attack	fight
enemies	people who want to do you harm people on the opposite side in a war
palace	grand home home for royalty
prisoner	person who has been captured captive
soldiers	members of an army warriors
strong	hard to break mighty

Read each sentence and look at the underlined word. Write the Key Word that means the same as the underlined word or words. Use the chart to help you.

1. A king and queen lived in a grand home. _____

2. People who wanted to do them harm planned to attack the palace. _____

3. The warriors were ready to fight. _____

4. One morning, the king's enemies planned to fight the warriors. _____

5. The walls of the city were hard to break and held back the king's enemies. _____

6. The king's army did not take even one captive. _____

54 Unit 2 Hidden Forces

READING STRATEGY

Use with textbook page 59.

Problems and Solutions

When you read a story, think about the problem the characters in the story face and the solution they find.

Underline the sentence that answers each question about "The Trojan Horse."

1. What problem did Queen Helen have?
   a. She was held prisoner by the Trojans.
   b. She had run away to Troy.

2. What problem did the Greeks have?
   a. The Greeks wanted Queen Helen to stay in Troy.
   b. The Greeks wanted to get into Troy and take Queen Helen home.

3. How did the Greeks try to solve their problem?
   a. They forgot all about Queen Helen and did not miss her.
   b. They attacked Troy many times, but the walls were too strong.

4. Who gave Odysseus the idea to trick the Trojans?
   a. Athena gave him the idea.
   b. A Trojan soldier gave him the idea.

5. How did the Greeks finally solve their problem?
   a. They used very high ladders to climb the high walls.
   b. They tricked their enemies by riding into the city inside a huge wooden horse.

Unit 2   Hidden Forces

Name _____ Date _____

VOCABULARY BUILDING
Use after the vocabulary lesson.

Understanding Compound Words
A **compound word** is formed when two words are joined together to make a new word.

story teller	storyteller
moon light	moonlight
earth quake	earthquake

Find the underlined compound word in each sentence. Then write the two words that form that compound word.

1. Queen Helen was in the <u>faraway</u> land of Troy.
   _____ _____

2. Helen's husband traveled by <u>sailboat</u> to get her.
   _____ _____

3. His soldiers camped <u>outside</u> the walls of the city.
   _____ _____

4. They built a wooden horse and went to hide <u>inside</u>.
   _____ _____

5. After <u>sunset</u>, the Greeks climbed in.
   _____ _____

6. By the next <u>afternoon</u>, the horse was through the gates.
   _____ _____

7. At night, the Greeks went out the <u>doorway</u>.
   _____ _____

8. <u>Everyone</u> was glad when Queen Helen was saved.
   _____ _____

Name _____ Date _____

PHONICS

Use after the phonics lesson.

Short *i*, *o*, and *u*

The letters *i*, *o*, and *u* often stand for short vowel sounds.

Short *i* is the middle sound you hear in the word *ship*.

Short *o* is the middle sound you hear in the word *box*.

Short *u* is the middle sound you hear in the word *sun*.

▲ ship

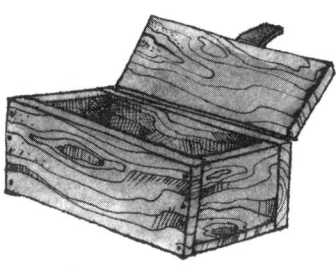
▲ box

▲ sun

Read the words for each vowel sound in this chart. Write a rhyming word next to each word.

Short *i*	Short *o*	Short *u*
1. hit _____	5. pot _____	9. bud _____
2. tin _____	6. mop _____	10. sun _____
3. lid _____	7. dog _____	11. dug _____
4. hip _____	8. sob _____	12. pup _____

Read the words in the box below. Use the words to answer the riddles.

| big   rug   pin   fox |

13. I have the same vowel sound as *lid*.
    I rhyme with *tin*.
    I am used to hold things together.
    What am I?

    I am a _____ .

14. I have the same vowel sound as *mop*.
    I rhyme with *box*.
    I live in a den.
    What am I?

    I am a _____ .

15. I have the same vowel sound as *sun*.
    I rhyme with *dug*.
    I cover part of a floor.
    What am I?

    I am a _____ .

16. I have the same vowel sound as *hip*.
    I rhyme with *pig*.
    I am the opposite of *little*.
    What am I?

    I am _____ .

Unit 2   Hidden Forces

Name _____ Date _____

PHONICS

Use after the phonics lesson.

Review Consonants c and g

The letter c can stand for two different sounds: /s/ and /k/. When c is followed by *a, o, u, r,* or *l,* it has the same first sound as *cat* (/k/).

    carry   **c**oat   **c**up   **c**runch   **c**limbed

When c is followed by *i, e,* or *y,* it has the same first sound as *circle* (/s/).

    citizen   **c**ell   pala**c**e   **c**yberspace

Read each word and think about the sound the letter c stands for. Write each word under the correct heading in the chart below.

    center   de**c**orate   pla**c**e   de**c**ide
    curious   se**c**ret   **c**amped   ni**c**e

c has the same sound as c in *cat* (/k/)	c has the same sound as c in *city* (/s/)
1.	5.
2.	6.
3.	7.
4.	8.

The letter g can stand for two different sounds: /g/ and /j/. Sometimes the letter g has the same first sound as *goat* (/g/).

    gift   si**g**nal   bi**g**

Sometimes the letter g has the same first sound as *gem* (/j/).

    gym   hu**g**e   **g**iant

Read each word and think about the sound the letter g stands for. Write each word under the correct heading in the chart below.

    gel   lar**g**e   **G**reeks   pa**g**e
    generous   **g**ates   du**g**   be**g**in

g has the same sound as g in *goat* (/g/)	g has the same sound as g in *gem* (/j/)
9.	13.
10.	14.
11.	15.
12.	16.

Name _____ Date _____

COMPREHENSION

Use with textbook page 64.

"The Trojan Horse"
Write a word from the box to complete each sentence about "The Trojan Horse."

beautiful	trick	prisoner	attacked	gates
city	horse	secret	inside	strong

Helen was the _____ queen of the Greeks. A Trojan prince made her
           1.

a _____ . The walls of Troy were very _____ . The Greeks
    2.   3.

_____ many times, but they could not save their queen.
   4.

The Greeks decided to build a wooden _____ . There was a place to
                                         5.

hide _____ the horse. Odysseus and twenty soldiers were hidden
       6.

inside.

The Trojans were curious about the huge horse. One Trojan warned that the horse

was a _____ . But the Trojans pulled the horse through the gates into
        7.

the _____ .
       8.

Queen Helen guessed the Greek soldiers were inside the horse, but she kept the

_____ . Late that night, the Greeks soldiers came out of the horse. They
    9.

opened the _____ of the city and saved Queen Helen.
              10.

Use cursive writing to write the last paragraph above that tells about the night Queen
Helen was saved.

_____

_____

_____

_____

_____

Unit 2   Hidden Forces

Name _____ Date _____

SKILLS FOR WRITING

Writing Descriptive Sentences
A **descriptive sentence** helps a reader visualize how someone or something looks, acts, or feels.

    The city was peaceful.

What is being described?   *the city*
How does it look?   *peaceful*

    There was beautiful Queen Helen.

What is being described?   *Queen Helen*
How does she look?   *beautiful*

Underline the person, place, or thing being described in each sentence. Then write the descriptive sentence.

1. Queen Helen was feeling unsafe and lonely.
   _____

2. The city walls were high and strong.
   _____

3. Odysseus was very clever.
   _____

4. The wooden horse was huge.
   _____

5. Flowers as bright as sunshine were gathered.
   _____

6. Fearless soldiers hid inside the horse.
   _____

7. Queen Helen was grateful to be going home.
   _____

8. This fascinating story has been told for centuries.
   _____

Name _____ Date _____

SPELLING

Use after the spelling lesson.

Short i, o, and u

Some words have the **consonant-vowel-consonant** spelling pattern called C-V-C. These C-V-C words have short *i*, short *o*, or short *u*.

Short *i*		Short *o*		Short *u*	
big	*big*	top	*top*	nut	*nut*
hid	*hid*	not	*not*	but	*but*
did	*did*	got	*got*	dug	*dug*
dip	*dip*	jog	*jog*	gum	*gum*

Circle the C-V-C word in each sentence. Print the word. Then write the word in cursive.

1. Helen could not escape from Troy. _____ _____
2. The Greeks did a clever thing. _____ _____
3. They made a big wooden horse. _____ _____
4. Greek soldiers hid in the horse. _____ _____
5. The Trojans were brave but foolish. _____ _____
6. The Greeks got Helen back. _____ _____

Write two words from the box to answer each question.

tug hot lit fun lot hug hit sun

7. Which two words rhyme with *rug*? _____ and _____
8. Which two words rhyme with *not*? _____ and _____
9. Which two words rhyme with *fit*? _____ and _____
10. Which two words rhyme with *run*? _____ and _____

Write two rhyming pairs in cursive.

11. _____ and _____
12. _____ and _____

Unit 2   Hidden Forces

Name _____ Date _____

VOCABULARY

Use with textbook page 67.

"Earthquakes"

Key Words		
crust	dangerous	destroy
directions	plates	powerful

▲ a powerful force

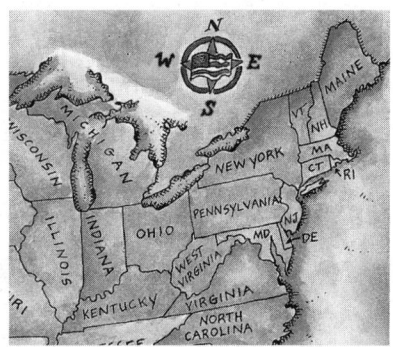
▲ directions on a map

▲ destroyed buildings

Circle the Key Word in each sentence.

1. The earth's crust is its hard outer part.
2. Plates are drifting pieces of rock that are part of the earth's surface.
3. A powerful force can move a heavy object.
4. Something that is dangerous may be harmful or hurtful.
5. To destroy means to ruin completely.
6. Directions are the way things move or point.

Write each sentence that is true.

    A fire can destroy a home.
    A fire cannot destroy a home.

7. _____

    A very strong wind can be a powerful force.
    A very light wind can be a powerful force.

8. _____

    A little rain is dangerous in a city.
    An earthquake is dangerous in a city.

9. _____

Name _____ Date _____

READING STRATEGY

Use with textbook page 67.

Cause and Effect
Why something happens is a **cause**. What happens is an **effect**.

Read the text and look at the pictures on pages 68 and 69 in your book.

1. Write the title of the article. It is in big capital letters on page 68.

   Title: _____

2. Read these sentences that tell why an earthquake happens.

   Causes
   Plates meet and press together.
   Pressure builds between the plates.
   One plate snaps past the other plate.
   The snap causes the rock around it to shake.

   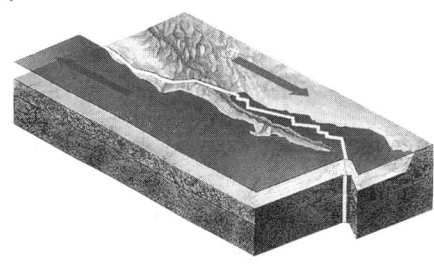

   Write the last two sentences you just read.

   _____

   _____

Read the question and the sentences. Underline the correct answer. Then write the sentence.

3. What is an earthquake?

   a. An earthquake is a sudden shaking of the ground.

   b. An earthquake is thunder and lightning.

   _____

   _____

4. What effect might a powerful earthquake have?

   a. A powerful earthquake might cause a terrible rainstorm.

   b. A powerful earthquake might cause buildings to fall.

   _____

   _____

Unit 2   Hidden Forces

Name _____ Date _____

GRAMMAR

Use with textbook page 74.

Simple Past: Regular Verbs
A **verb** shows an action or state of being. Use the **simple past** to talk about an action that happened in the past and is completed.

    The earthquake **lasted** for a few minutes.

For **regular verbs**, add -ed to the base form of the verb to show the simple past.

talk + ed	talked	happen + ed	happened

For verbs that end with -e, add -d to form the simple past.

quake + d	quaked	change + d	changed

Underline the simple past form of the verb in each sentence.

1. My class learned about earthquakes in school.
2. We shared books about earthquakes.
3. Last month I visited my friend in California.
4. We listened to a TV reporter.
5. He reported news about a nearby earthquake.

Complete each sentence with the simple past form of the verb.

6. Last year my family (travel) _____ to San Francisco.
7. We (walk) _____ around a famous science center.
8. I (use) _____ a toy to model earthquake waves.
9. I (push) _____ the toy to make it shake.
10. It (vibrate) _____ in different directions.
11. I (learn) _____ a lot about earthquakes that day.
12. I (like) _____ doing things at the science center.
13. My mom (promise) _____ we could visit again.

Unit 2   Hidden Forces

GRAMMAR

Use after the grammar lesson.

Understanding Adjectives

An **adjective** is a word that describes a noun. A noun names a person, place, or thing.

> a **sad** woman   a **busy** city   a **terrible** earthquake

Underline the adjective in each sentence below. Then write the noun it describes.

1. Strong plates move slowly.   _____
2. The enormous pressure builds.   _____
3. Soon there are huge cracks.   _____
4. A powerful earthquake comes.   _____
5. The solid ground shakes and crumbles. _____
6. Tall buildings fall quickly to the ground. _____

Complete each sentence with an adjective from the box that describes the underlined noun.

> | different | tall | special | small |
> | big | powerful | famous | interesting |

7. I read an _____ article about earthquakes.
8. Earthquakes can be mild or very _____ .
9. Plates in the earth's crust move in _____ directions.
10. Scientists measure earthquakes with _____ machines.
11. Their machines can measure _____ waves.
12. Their machines can record _____ waves, too.
13. Earthquakes can destroy _____ buildings.
14. The San Andreas Fault is a _____ fault.

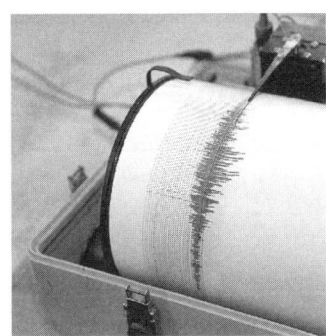

Unit 2   Hidden Forces

COMPREHENSION

Use with textbook page 72.

"Earthquakes"
Write a word from the box to complete each sentence about "Earthquakes."

| rock | earthquake | shake | little |
| fault | snaps | crust | dangerous |

You may be surprised to learn that an earthquake lasts only seconds or minutes. In that short time, an _____ can cause great damage. A powerful
            1.
earthquake can be a very dangerous thing. A mild earthquake may cause

_____ or no damage.
     2.

The earth's crust is a layer of rock that covers the earth. The earth's crust is made

of huge pieces of _____ called plates. An earthquake happens when
                         3.
these plates meet and press together. Slowly pressure builds between the plates. Then

one of the plates _____ past the other plate. The powerful snap causes
                         4.
the ground around it to _____. That sudden shaking of the ground is an
                                  5.
earthquake. During an earthquake, the earth's _____ cracks. The cracks
                                                              6.
are called faults.

One famous _____ is the San Andreas Fault in California.
                    7.
Earthquakes along this fault happen close to the earth's surface. They are more

_____ than earthquakes that happen deep under the surface.
      8.

Write the paragraph above that tells about the San Andreas Fault.

_____

_____

_____

_____

_____

Name _____ Date _____

SPELLING PATTERNS

Use after the spelling lesson.

in, id, on, ot, un, ud

Complete each word with the spelling patterns *in*, *id*, *on*, *ot*, *un*, and *ud*.

in	on	un
pr___ ___ce	h___ ___ored	f___ ___ny
___ ___to	g___ ___e	___ ___der
br___ ___g	Poseid___ ___	s___ ___ny
id	**ot**	**ud**
h___ ___den	sp___ ___ted	m___ ___
d___ ___	forg___ ___	s___ ___den
sl___ ___	pl___ ___	th___ ___

Read each sentence. Find the correct word from the chart and fill in the missing letters.

1. Write the word that begins with *br*. ___ ___in ___

2. Write the word that names a king's son. ___ ___in ___ ___

3. Write the word that ends with *o*. in ___ ___

4. Write the word that begins with *sl*. ___ ___id

5. Write the word that means *not here anymore*. ___on ___

6. Write the word that rhymes with *sunny*. ___un ___ ___

7. Write the word that rhymes with *thud*. ___ud

8. Write the word that begins with *pl*. ___ ___ot

Unit 2   Hidden Forces

Name _____   Date _____

GRAMMAR

Use with textbook page 74.

Present and Past Tense: Irregular Verbs
Some verbs are **irregular verbs**. An irregular verb does not follow the rules for regular verbs. Here are boxes to help you use four irregular verbs correctly.

be	
Present Tense	**Past Tense**
I **am**.	I **was**.
You **are**.	You **were**.
He **is**.	He **was**.
She **is**.	She **was**.
We **are**.	We **were**.
They **are**.	They **were**.

do	
Present Tense	**Past Tense**
I **do**.	I **did**.
You **do**.	You **did**.
He **does**.	He **did**.
She **does**.	She **did**.
We **do**.	We **did**.
They **do**.	They **did**.

say	
Present Tense	**Past Tense**
I **say**.	I **said**.
You **say**.	You **said**.
He **says**.	He **said**.
She **says**.	She **said**.
We **say**.	We **said**.
They **say**.	They **said**.

go	
Present Tense	**Past Tense**
I **go**.	I **went**.
You **go**.	You **went**.
He **goes**.	He **went**.
She **goes**.	She **went**.
We **go**.	We **went**.
They **go**.	They **went**.

Complete each sentence using the present tense of the verb.

1. Helen (be) _____ a beautiful queen.

2. She (do) _____ not want to be in Troy.

3. She (say) _____ , "I will wait for help."

4. Helen (go) _____ to watch for the Greeks.

Complete each sentence using the past tense of the verb.

5. Helen (be) _____ a beautiful queen.

6. She (do) _____ not want to be in Troy.

7. She (say) _____ , "I will wait for help."

8. Helen (go) _____ to watch for the Greeks.

Name _____ Date _____

VOCABULARY BUILDING

Use after the vocabulary lesson.

Understanding Phrasal Verbs

A **phrasal verb** is a two-word or three-word verb. It contains the main verb and at least one preposition. The meaning of a phrasal verb is different from the meaning of the verb alone.

To **call** has a different meaning from to **call off**.

    I **call** my friend to come over.   (to telephone someone)
    I **call off** the game when it rains.   (to decide an event will not happen)

Read the phrasal verbs and their meanings in the box below.

Phrasal Verbs	Meanings
figure out	plan carefully
work out	develop
check into	see; research
write down	list
get by	manage to be all right
count on	depend on
end up with	finish; conclude
go over	do again; review

Read each sentence. Look at the underlined phrasal verb. Then write its meaning. Use the box to help you.

1. You should <u>figure out</u> what to do in an emergency. _____

2. First, <u>work out</u> a plan with your family members. _____

3. You might <u>check into</u> plans other people make. _____

4. It's a good idea to <u>write down</u> things you will need. _____

5. You must have enough water, food, and batteries to <u>get by</u>. _____

6. You might list people you can <u>count on</u>. _____

7. You will <u>end up with</u> a helpful list. _____

8. <u>Go over</u> your list often and change it when needed. _____

Unit 2   Hidden Forces

Name _____ Date _____

SKILLS FOR WRITING

Use with textbook page 75.

Writing a Personal Narrative

A narrative tells a story. A **personal narrative** tells a story about an experience you had. You usually tell a personal narrative in the order that the events happened.

You can use sequence words to show the order of events. Sequence words usually come at the beginning of a sentence. Some sequence words are *first, next, then, after that,* and *finally.*

Read this personal narrative. Then answer the questions.

My Class Play

Last week, my class read "The Trojan Horse." We read the play, too. A girl in my class named Jenny suggested that we read the play to another class. I got the part of the narrator. It was just the part I wanted.

The day of the performance came. Unfortunately, I had the hiccups. I tried to stop my hiccups. First, I tried drinking water. Next, I tried holding my breath for thirty seconds. Nothing helped me.

After that, I did manage to read my lines, but with lots of hiccups. Finally it was over, and the audience clapped for us. I would like to do another performance. But I hope the next time I read without hiccups.

1. How do you know that this is a personal narrative?

   _____

   _____

2. What happened to the writer on the day of the performance?

   _____

   _____

3. What is the second paragraph mostly about?

   _____

   _____

4. Write the sequence words the writer used to show the order of events.

   _____   _____

   _____   _____

Name _____ Date _____

WRITING PRACTICE

Write About "Hidden Forces"
Think about what you read about in Unit 2.

Think about a Greek soldier hiding inside the huge wooden horse. How did he feel as he waited? What noises did he hear? Write three or more sentences about the Greek soldier in the wooden horse. Here are some words you might want to use.

attack	enemies	palace
prisoner	soldiers	strong

_____
_____
_____
_____

Think about a person in an earthquake. She just felt the ground shake. What did that feel like? What was the first question that came into her mind? Write three or more sentences about the person in the earthquake.

_____
_____
_____
_____

Unit 2   Hidden Forces

Name _____ Date _____

UNIT 3 Play Ball!

INTRODUCTION: LOOKING AHEAD

Use with textbook pages 78–80.

Here are the titles of the selections you will read. Complete the sentences below with the correct title.

> "The Bouncing Ball"   "Roberto Clemente"

1. The first selection I will read is about the history of the rubber ball.

   _____ is the title of that selection.

2. The next selection I will read is about a famous baseball player.

   _____ is the title of that selection.

Complete each sentence about the picture with a word from the box. Use printing and cursive writing.

> famous   bounce
> *famous*   *bounce*

3. Here is an ancient rubber ball.

   I will find out how the Aztec and Maya people made balls that

   could _____ .

   I will find out how the Aztec and Maya people made

   balls that could _____ .

4. Here are a baseball and glove.

   I will read about a _____ baseball player.

   I will read about a _____ *baseball player.*

72   Unit 3   Play Ball!

Name _____ Date _____

VOCABULARY

Use with textbook page 81.

"The Bouncing Ball"

Key Words
artifact   bounce   explorers   rubber   statue

▲ a statue of a ballplayer

▲ explorers on a ship

▲ ancient artifacts

Complete each sentence with a Key Word from the box. Use the pictures to help you.

1. People who explore far-off places are _____.

2. The material that makes balls bounce is _____.

3. A _____ is a figure of a person made from stone, clay, wood, metal, or wax.

4. An object that was made in ancient times is an _____.

5. To _____ means to hit a surface and spring back.

Write each sentence that is true.

   A statue moves all by itself.
   A statue can be made of stone.

6. _____

   An artifact is made by people.
   An artifact is made by animals.

7. _____

   Rubber comes from rubber trees.
   Rubber comes from the ocean.

8. _____

Unit 3   Play Ball!

Name _____ Date _____

EXTENDING VOCABULARY

Use with textbook page 81.

Using Key Words

A syllable has one vowel sound in it. Some words have one syllable. Some words have two syllables. Some have more. When you clap the rhythm of a word you say, you are clapping the syllables.

One Syllable (1 Clap)	Two Syllables (2 Claps)	Three Syllables (3 Claps)
bounce	rub′ber	ex·plor′ers
ball	stat′ue	ar′ti·fact
wood	bounc′ing	ball′play·er

You will see some of these words when you read "The Bouncing Ball." Choose a word from the chart to answer each riddle.

1. I am what a ball can do if it is made of rubber.

   I have one syllable. Which word am I? _____

2. I am a figure that can be made of stone.

   I have two syllables. Which word am I? _____

3. I am an object from the past that shows how people lived long ago.

   I have three syllables. Which word am I? _____

4. I am a word that means people who travel to explore new places.

   I have three syllables. Which word am I? _____

Circle the two-syllable word in each question. Then write the word.

5. Was the statue made of wood?   _____

6. Was the child's toy made of rubber?   _____

Circle the three-syllable word in each question. Then write the word.

7. Where did the explorers travel?   _____

8. Who found the artifacts?   _____

Name _____ Date _____

READING STRATEGY

Use with textbook page 81.

Ask Questions

Ask questions as you read. Stop to check your understanding. Ask yourself these kinds of questions:

- What is the text about?
- Does this text make sense?

Read the caption below the picture (right). Stop to ask yourself the questions. Write the answers. Ask yourself:

1. What are these sentences about?

   _____
   _____

2. What do I know about rubber?

   _____
   _____

3. What did I read that is new to me?

   _____
   _____

▲ Rubber comes from rubber trees. Balls made of rubber can bounce up and down.

▲ This statue of a Maya ballplayer is an artifact. An artifact is an object made by people. We learn about ancient peoples from the artifacts they have left behind.

Now read the caption below the picture (left). Ask yourself:

4. What is this player holding?

   _____
   _____

5. When was the statue made?

   _____
   _____

6. What did I read that is new to me?

   _____
   _____

Unit 3   Play Ball!

Name _____ Date _____

VOCABULARY BUILDING

Use after the lesson about the suffix -er.

Understanding the Suffix -er
A **suffix** is one or more letters that are added to the end of a base word. The letters -er can be a suffix. The suffix -er can change an action word to a word that names the person who does the action.

> travel + er = traveler   work + er = worker

Add -er to these words and write the new word.

1. play + er   _____

2. catch + er   _____

Underline the noun that names a person who does the action. Then use it to finish the next sentence.

3. A player is a person who plays ball.

   A Maya _____ put the ball through a stone ring.

4. A catcher is a person who catches.

   A baseball _____ catches the ball.

5. A jumper is a person who jumps.

   In basketball, a high _____ can slam dunk.

Complete each sentence with the noun that names the person who does the action. Add -er to the underlined action word to make the noun.

6. Bob will <u>play</u> a game of football.   Bob is a great _____.

7. Jan will <u>help</u> her mom.   Jan is her mom's _____.

8. Ed will <u>paint</u> my house.   Ed is a _____.

9. Pablo will <u>report</u> the news each day.   Pablo is a news _____.

10. Sara can <u>learn</u> quickly.   Sara is a fast _____.

11. Tom likes to <u>read</u> stories.   Tom is a good _____.

12. Alicia loves to <u>teach</u> children.   Alicia is a _____.

13. Sam can <u>catch</u> any fast ball.   Sam is a good _____.

Name _____ Date _____

PHONICS

Use after the phonics lesson.

Long Vowels with Signal e

These three-letter words with short vowel sounds follow a **consonant-vowel-consonant** pattern. This is called a **C-V-C** pattern.

cap   pet   bit   not   cub

When the pattern is **consonant-vowel-consonant-signal e**, the pattern is called a **C-V-C-e** pattern. The letter e in the pattern signals that the first vowel sound is long. Remember that the long vowel sound is the sound of the letter's name.

cap + e = cape	Pet + e = Pete	bit + e = bite
not + e = note	cub + e = cube	

Underline the word that follows a consonant-vowel-consonant-signal e pattern in each sentence about a boy named Pete. Then write the word.

1. Pete went to the library to get a book.   _____

2. He found five good books.   _____

3. He took home a really interesting book.   _____

4. The book gave facts about the history of sports.   _____

5. The book is due back on June 3.   _____

Write a word from the chart to complete each sentence about Pete and Gene.

Long a	Long e	Long i	Long o
game	Pete	side	home
gave	Gene	like	notes

6. Pete has a friend named _____ .

7. Pete and Gene _____ to play baseball.

8. Pete hits a _____ run in every game.

9. The team _____ Pete a prize for most home runs.

Unit 3   Play Ball!

Name _____ Date _____

PHONICS

Use after the phonics lesson.

Review y as /y/, Long e, and Long i

The letter *y* can stand for different sounds. When *y* is at the beginning of a word or syllable, it stands for the same first sound as *yes*.

    you   **y**oung   **y**ellow   **y**ard

Sometimes *y* stands for the long *e* sound.

    funn**y**   happ**y**   man**y**   prett**y**

Sometimes *y* stands for the long *i* sound.

    fl**y**   t**y**pe   dr**y**   m**y**self

Think about the sound the letter *y* stands for in each word in the box. Write each word under the correct heading in the chart below.

| try | city | yet | your | history |
| by | yell | why | baby | |

y stands for the same sound as *y* in *yes*	y stands for the same sound as *y* in *funny*	y stands for the same sound as *y* in *fly*
1. _____	4. _____	7. _____
2. _____	5. _____	8. _____
3. _____	6. _____	9. _____

Find and write the two words in each sentence that have the letter *y*.

    You read some information about the history of the bouncing ball.

10. _____ _____

    It would be fun to make a list of the many types of balls used for sports.

11. _____ _____

Unit 3   Play Ball!

Name _____   Date _____

COMPREHENSION

Use with textbook page 86.

"The Bouncing Ball"
Complete each sentence about "The Bouncing Ball" with a word from the box.

wood	rubber	ring	court	explorers
bounce	games	teams	pads	two

Before the 1500s, Europeans played games with balls made of leather or _____**1.**_____ . The balls they used could not _____**2.**_____ . In the early 1500s, Spanish _____**3.**_____ went to Central America. There, they met the Aztecs and Mayas, who played games with balls made of _____**4.**_____ . Artifacts from that time tell us about the games they played. One game was played with two _____**5.**_____ of players. These players tried to bounce a ball through a _____**6.**_____ .

Spanish explorers took some rubber balls back to Europe. People there loved the new kind of ball and they loved to play the new ball _____**7.**_____ .

Many games that we play today come from those games. Just like those games, we play ball games on a _____**8.**_____ or a field. In many games, _____**9.**_____ teams play against each other. Sometimes the players wear _____**10.**_____ to protect themselves.

Write the sentences that tell why Europeans began to use a new kind of ball. Use cursive writing.

_____

_____

_____

_____

_____

Unit 3   Play Ball!

Name _____ Date _____

SKILLS FOR WRITING

Writing Questions and Answers

A sentence that asks a question begins with a **capital letter** and ends with a **question mark**.

   Question: **W**ho played in the ball games**?**

Some questions begin with these question words: *Who, What, When, Where, Why, How.*

Complete each sentence about the history of the rubber ball. Choose a question word from the box to begin each sentence. Begin each sentence with a capital letter and end with a question mark.

Who   What   When   Where   Why   How

1. _____ did European explorers come to Central America ___

2. _____ strange new kind of ball did they see ___

3. _____ do rubber balls bounce ___

4. _____ found artifacts in Mexico ___

5. _____ did scientists find clay statues ___

6. _____ are our games today like ancient games

A sentence that answers a question begins with a **capital letter** and ends with a **period**.

   Question: **W**ho played in the ball games**?**
   Answer: **T**he Mayas and Aztecs played in the ball games**.**

Choose one question from above and write it below. Then write your answer to the question.

7. Question:

   _____

   Answer:

   _____

80 Unit 3 Play Ball!

Name _____ Date _____

SPELLING

Use after the phonics lesson.

Initial and Final y

Remember, the letter *y* can stand for different sounds. When *y* is at the beginning of a word or syllable, it stands for the same first sound as *yes*.

    yell   **y**am

Sometimes *y* stands for the long *e* sound.

    sunn**y**   an**y**

Sometimes *y* stands for the long *i* sound.

    sk**y**   wh**y**

Read the words in the box.

country	try	your	history	sky	yellow
sunny	yard	study	yet	July	fry

Write the four words that begin with the letter *y*.

1. _____ 3. _____

2. _____ 4. _____

Write the four words that end with long *i* spelled with the letter *y*.

5. _____ 7. _____

6. _____ 8. _____

Write the four words that end with long *e* spelled with the letter *y*.

9. _____ 11. _____

10. _____ 12. _____

Now write a rhyming word for each of the following words.

13. funny _____

14. why _____

15. set _____

Unit 3   Play Ball!

VOCABULARY

Use with textbook page 89.

"Roberto Clemente"

Key Words
achievements   medicine   opportunity   rescue   supplies

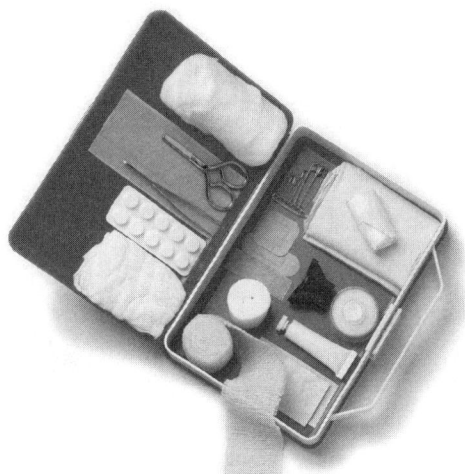
▲ medical supplies

▲ art supplies

Circle the Key Word in each sentence.

1. Achievements are results that people work hard for.
2. An opportunity is a chance to achieve something.
3. To rescue means to save from danger.
4. Medicine is used to help sick people get well.
5. Supplies are things people need.

Read each sentence. Then write *Yes* if the sentence is correct. Write *No* if the sentence is not correct.

6. Climbing a mountain is not an achievement. _____
7. Roberto helped people who were in need. _____
8. People who rescue others are never called heroes. _____
9. Supplies for a hospital may be bandages, medicine, and food. _____
10. Medicine should be given to a child by a parent or doctor. _____

Name _____ Date _____

READING STRATEGY

Use with textbook page 89.

Understand Chronological Order

Writers usually organize events in chronological, or time, order. **Chronological order** is the time order in which events occur. Writers use time phrases such as *the next day, 1972,* or *March 23* to show this kind of order.

- Try to find the time phrases in the text you read.
- Make a T-chart to help you remember dates and events.
- Place dates on the left side and events on the right side of the T-chart.

The following are facts from the life of Roberto Clemente.

In 1971, Roberto helped the Pirates win the World Series.	Roberto began playing minor league baseball in 1953.
Roberto joined the Pittsburgh Pirates in 1954.	In 1973, Roberto was elected to the Baseball Hall of Fame.
Roberto died in 1972.	Roberto was born in 1934.

Write each fact next to the correct year in the T-chart below.

Date	Event in Roberto Clemente's Life
1934	
1953	
1954	
1971	
1972	
1973	

Unit 3 Play Ball!

Name _____ Date _____

GRAMMAR

Use after the grammar lesson.

Questions in the Present

Present Tense of the Verb *to do*	
Do I want to play ball?	**Do we** want to play ball?
Do you want to play ball?	**Do they** want to play ball?
Does he want to play ball?	
Does she want to play ball?	

Complete the question sentences below with the present tense of the verb *to do*. Use the box above to help you.

I am a big fan of the game of baseball. _____ you want to know how
                                          1.
much I love the game? Today my team is at a big league game. The Pittsburgh Pirates
are playing. _____ we want them to win? We do! And how
               2.
_____ the Pirates feel? _____ they want to win? Yes!
  3.   **4.**
_____ each batter want to hit a home run? Yes!
  5.

Present Tense of the Verb *to be*	
Am I on the team?	**Are we** on the team?
Are you on the team?	**Are they** on the team?
Is he on the team?	
Is she on the team?	

Complete these question sentences with the present tense of the verb *to be*. Use the box above to help you.

It is the ninth inning. _____ I excited? _____ the
                          6.   **7.**
players on my team excited? You bet we are!

The score is 4 to 4. The best Pirate hitter comes up to the plate.
_____ he going to hit a home run? _____ the Pirates
  8.   **9.**
going to win? _____ we going to yell and cheer if he hits a homer?
                10.
Strike one! Strike two! All the Pirates fans are standing up and yelling. So am I. So are
my teammates. He hits the ball. See ya! The game is over, 5 to 4!

_____ I happy? Do you have to ask?
  11.

84   Unit 3   Play Ball!

Name _____ Date _____

GRAMMAR

Use after the grammar lesson.

Proper Nouns

A **proper noun** names a specific person, place, or thing. Proper nouns always begin with a capital letter.

Some proper nouns name specific people.

    Roberto Clemente   "The Great One"

Some proper nouns name specific places.

    Nicaragua   Central America   United States   Baseball Hall of Fame

Some proper nouns name specific things.

    December (month)   Pittsburgh Pirates (team)
    English (language)   "The Great One" (title)

Rewrite each sentence with the proper nouns capitalized.

1. The brooklyn dodgers was the name of a baseball team.

   _____

2. People in nicaragua, in central america, needed help.

   _____

3. On new year's eve, Roberto Clemente's plane went down.

   _____

4. roberto clemente was killed in the crash.

   _____

5. Roberto Clemente is in the baseball hall of fame.

   _____

6. The pittsburgh pirates won the world series.

   _____

7. Roberto Clemente was called "the great one."

   _____

Circle the nouns that are written correctly.

8. Pennsylvania   11. Artifacts   14. Brooklyn Dodgers

9. hero   12. Mexico   15. spanish

10. united states   13. aztecs   16. most valuable player

Name _____ Date _____

COMPREHENSION
Use with textbook page 94.

"Roberto Clemente"
Complete each sentence about "Roberto Clemente" with a word or phrase from the box.

| ocean | medicine | earthquake | eighteen | Pittsburgh Pirates |
| Nicaragua | baseball | Puerto Rico | elected | "The Great One" |

Roberto Clemente was born in _____**1.**_____ . He became a great _____**2.**_____ player. He played for the _____**3.**_____ team for _____**4.**_____ years, starting in 1954. He was more than a baseball hero. He helped many people. He was called _____**5.**_____ .

In December 1972, there was an _____**6.**_____ in _____**7.**_____ . Supplies were needed. Rescue workers needed more _____**8.**_____ . Roberto and his friends took a plane to Nicaragua. The plane had problems. It went down in the _____**9.**_____ . All of the people on the plane died. Soon after, Roberto was _____**10.**_____ to the Baseball Hall of Fame.

Answer the questions. Use cursive writing.

11. Where was Roberto Clemente born?
_____

12. What team did Roberto Clemente play on in 1954?
_____

13. Where was Roberto Clemente going when his plane went down?
_____

14. What special name did people give to Roberto Clemente?
_____

86   Unit 3   Play Ball!

Name _____   Date _____

SPELLING PATTERNS

Use after the phonics lesson.

Long Vowels with Signal e

A word that has a **consonant-vowel-consonant-signal e** pattern is called a **C-V-C-e** pattern. The **signal e** signals that the first vowel is long.

> mak**e**   Pet**e**   bik**e**   hom**e**   tub**e**

In these C-V-C-e words, the vowel sound is long *a*. Complete each word with the letter *a* and signal *e*.

1. c __ p __
2. pl __ n __
3. l __ k __

Now use one of the words to complete each sentence.

4. I flew in a _____ called an Airbus.
5. Our cabin is on a _____ .
6. I wear a _____ instead of a coat.

In these C-V-C-e words, the vowel sound is long *o*. Complete each word with the letter *o* and signal *e*.

7. h __ m __
8. ph __ n __
9. r __ p __

Now use one of the words to complete each sentence.

10. I will call you on my cell _____ .
11. I will be _____ at seven o'clock.
12. Our boat is tied with a long _____ .

In these C-V-C-e words, the vowel sound is long *i*. Complete each word with the letter *i* and signal *e*.

13. k __ t __
14. wr __ t __
15. l __ k __

Now use one of the words to complete each sentence.

16. I _____ to play baseball.
17. Our _____ flew away on the wind.
18. I like to _____ stories.

Unit 3   Play Ball!

Name _____ Date _____

GRAMMAR

Use with textbook page 96.

Questions

Questions may have parts that follow a special order. Here are some examples:

Question Word	*did*	Subject	Verb	Question Mark
When	did	Roberto	play	?
Why	did	the people	cheer	?
Who	did	Roberto	help	?
What	did	his friends	do	?
Where	did	Roberto	go	?
How	did	the game	end	?

Write the words in the correct order to make a question.

1. did go the people Where ? _____
2. find the explorers What did ? _____
3. When the team did win ? _____
4. did Why fly Roberto ? _____
5. Roberto travel Where did ? _____
6. the ball bounce did How ? _____

Write the question from the box below to match each answer.

> How many teams were there?
> How did they hit the ball?
> Where did the ball bounce?

7. _____

   They used different parts of their bodies to hit the ball.

8. _____

   The ball bounced through a ring.

9. _____

   There were two teams.

88   Unit 3   Play Ball!

VOCABULARY BUILDING

Use after the vocabulary lesson.

Suffix -ly

A **suffix** is one or more letters that are added to the end of a base word. A word that ends with the suffix -ly tells *how* something was done. Words that end with the suffix -ly are adverbs. They add meaning to a verb.

Complete the chart.

Verb	How?	Adverb
ran	quick + ly =	quick
walked	slow + ly =	slow
spoke	quiet + ly =	quiet
cheered	loud + ly =	loud
waved	proud + ly =	proud
hit	light + ly =	light

Look at the underlined verb in each sentence. Complete each sentence with a word that ends with the suffix -ly. Use the words from the chart.

1. The batter hit the ball _____, but it went far.

2. The player ran _____ around the bases.

3. The people cheered _____ when she hit a home run.

4. She won the game and waved _____ to the crowd.

5. They took their time and walked _____ to their seats.

6. The coach spoke so _____ that he could not be heard.

Write a sentence using a word that ends with the suffix -ly. Choose the word from the chart.

7. _____

_____

Unit 3   Play Ball!   89

SKILLS FOR WRITING

Use with textbook page 97.

Biographical Narrative

A **biographical narrative** tells the true story of a real person's life. Sometimes it includes a problem that the person had to solve. Writers usually tell events in a biographical narrative in chronological order—in the order that they happened.

Read this biographical narrative of the life of baseball player Babe Ruth.

Babe Ruth

Babe Ruth was one of the greatest hitters in the history of baseball. He was born in 1895, in Baltimore, Maryland.

In 1914, Babe Ruth began playing baseball on minor league teams. Next he joined a major league team, the Boston Red Sox. While he played for the Red Sox, he was a very good pitcher. Batters got few hits when he was pitching. He was also a very good batter.

In 1920 Babe Ruth joined the New York Yankees. He played for the Yankees for the rest of his career. In his life, he hit 715 home runs. His record was unbroken for many years. When the Baseball Hall of Fame was started, he was among the first five players to be chosen for it. He died in 1948, in New York.

Write the sentence from the biographical narrative that answers each question.

1. When and where was Babe Ruth born?
___

2. What happened in 1920?
___

3. How many home runs did Babe Ruth hit?
___

Name _____ Date _____

WRITING PRACTICE

Use with textbook page 98.

Write about "Play Ball!"
Think about what you read in Unit 3.

What facts did you learn about the history of the rubber ball? Write three or more sentences about Aztec and Maya ball games. Here are some words you might want to use.

| artifact | bounce | rubber | Central America |
| statue | explorers | Spain | |

_____
_____
_____
_____
_____
_____
_____

Plan a speech about Roberto Clemente. Write three or more facts you will tell people about him in your speech. Here are some words you might want to use.

| achievements | medicine | rescue | opportunity |
| "The Great One" | Nicaraguan | Most Valuable Player | |

_____
_____
_____
_____
_____
_____

Unit 3   Play Ball!

Name _____ Date _____

UNIT 4 Family Ties

INTRODUCTION: LOOKING AHEAD

Use with textbook pages 100–102.

Read this paragraph. It describes the first selection in Unit 4.

> In "The Clever Daughter-in-Law," a father wants his three sons to marry. The story has a riddle, or puzzle, in it. One girl answers the riddle and surprises everyone.

Answer the following questions about this paragraph.

1. What is the title of the first selection in this unit?

_____

2. How many sons does the father have?

_____

3. How does the girl surprise everyone?

_____

Read this paragraph. It describes the second selection in this unit.

> Grandparents, parents, and children often have many things in common. Their eye color or hair color may be the same. "Family Traits" tells about how people in families are alike.

Answer the following questions about this paragraph.

4. What is the title of the second selection that is described above?

_____

_____

5. What are two things parents and children may have in common?

_____

_____

Name _____ Date _____

VOCABULARY

Use with textbook page 103.

"The Clever Daughter-in-Law"

Key Words
clever   daughter-in-law   father-in-law   lantern   missed

◀ The father-in-law talks to his daughter-in-law.

▲ A Chinese lantern is made of paper.

Complete each sentence with a Key Word from the box. Use the pictures to help you.

1. A wife is the _____ of her husband's parents.

2. A _____ person knows a lot and is wise.

3. If someone is _____, you want to visit that person soon.

4. A woman's _____ is the father of her husband.

5. A _____ is a light that has a see-through covering.

Write each sentence that is true.

   A person who is clever is very foolish.
   A person who is clever is very smart.

6. _____

   A daughter-in-law is the sister of a man's son.
   A daughter-in-law is the wife of someone's son.

7. _____

   A lantern can be used to light the way.
   A lantern can be used to clean the house.

8. _____

Unit 4   Family Ties

Name _____ Date _____

EXTENDING VOCABULARY

Use with textbook page 103.

Using Key Words

A **noun** is a word that names a person, place, or thing. A **verb** is a word that describes an action. An **adjective** is a word that describes a noun.

      adjective noun   verb
  The **young sisters played** together.

Write each Key Word where it belongs in the chart below.

Key Words
clever   daughter-in-law   father-in-law   lantern   missed

Nouns	Verbs	Adjectives
gift	laughed	happy
_____	visited	old
_____	traveled	pretty
_____	_____	_____

Read the sentence. Read the word below the blank. Write the word from the chart that belongs in the blank.

1. The father of a woman's husband is her _____ .
                                                  (noun)

2. Because the daughter _____ her mother, she cried a lot.
                            (verb)

3. The _____ lit the dark night.
        (noun)

4. A _____ person may know all the answers.
     (adjective)

5. The woman's young _____ gave her a gift.
                      (noun)

6. The two women _____ down the road.
                  (verb)

Name _____ Date _____

READING STRATEGY

Use with textbook page 103.

Predict
To **predict** as you read means to guess what will happen.

- Look for story clues.
- Think about what is most likely to happen next.
- Use your own knowledge and experience.

Read this passage from the folktale "The Clever Daughter-in-Law" and predict what will happen.

> Two of the sons found lovely wives. The two wives were sisters from a family in the next town. Soon the sisters came to live in the big house with their new husbands and their father-in-law. The old man was very happy. But he still needed to find a wife for his third son.
>
> The two sisters liked the big new house, but they missed their mother terribly.

1. Underline the words that tell how the sisters felt about their mother.

2. What do you think the sisters will do? Circle your prediction.
   a. Write a letter to their mother.
   b. Go to visit their mother.

Now read this passage and predict what will happen.

> Soon a young farm girl saw them. She was walking with her water buffalo. "Why are you crying?" she asked. The sisters told her of the gifts they needed for their father-in-law.

3. Underline the words that tell what animal the girl was walking with.

4. What do you think might happen next? Circle your prediction.
   a. The girl will help the wives get the gifts.
   b. The girl will start to cry, too.

Unit 4   Family Ties   95

Name _____ Date _____

VOCABULARY BUILDING

Use after the vocabulary lesson.

Words That Tell When

Some **adverbs** tell *when*. Use adverbs that tell *when* to answer questions that begin with "When."

> Question: **When** are you going to see your mother?
> Answer: I am going to see her **later**.

Read each question. Complete each answer by choosing a word from the box that tells *when*. Use a different adverb in each sentence. More than one adverb may be correct. Not all adverbs will be used.

today	tomorrow	now	never
yesterday	next	early	before
sometimes	often	tonight	later
soon	finally		

1. Question: When will you read the story?

   Answer: I will read the story _____ .

2. Question: When did they marry?

   Answer: They married _____ .

3. Question: When will she make the lantern?

   Answer: She will make the lantern _____ .

4. Question: When will you wrap this present?

   Answer: I will wrap it _____ .

5. Question: When will she talk to her father-in-law?

   Answer: She will talk to her father-in-law _____ .

6. Question: When will you visit your cousin?

   Answer: I will visit my cousin _____ .

7. Question: When did he leave to go fishing?

   Answer: He left the night _____ .

8. Question: When will she get bored with dancing?

   Answer: She will _____ get bored with dancing.

Name _____   Date _____

PHONICS

Use after the phonics lesson.

Initial, Medial, Final Digraphs /ch/, /sh/, /th/

The letters *ch* stand for the sound /ch/ as in these words.

chicken   bran**ch**es   mu**ch**

The letters *sh* stand for the sound /sh/ as in these words.

ship   pu**sh**ed   fi**sh**

The letters *th* stand for two sounds, one voiced and one not voiced. Read these words and listen for the two sounds *th* can spell.

think   fa**th**er   wi**th**

Complete each sentence with a word from the lists in the box. Use the hint to help you.

/ch/	/sh/	/th/
rich	wishes	three
China	she	third
chocolate	shocked	mother
such	splashes	father

1. The folktale I read is from (/ch/) _____ .

2. The first two sons are married, but the (/th/) _____ is not.

3. The (/th/) _____ wants his third son to marry.

4. The sisters miss their (/th/) _____ .

5. The (/ch/) _____ old man asks for two gifts.

6. The sisters are (/sh/) _____ by the gifts the old man wants.

7. The young farm girl is (/ch/) _____ a clever woman.

8. The girl says that (/sh/) _____ will give the sisters two gifts.

9. The third son (/sh/) _____ to marry the clever girl.

10. At the end of the story all (/th/) _____ sons are married.

Unit 4   Family Ties

PHONICS

Use after the phonics lesson.

x /ks/, qu /kw/, wh /hw/

The letter x stands for /ks/, the sound you hear at the end of these words.

    bo**x**   fo**x**   si**x**

The letters qu stand for /kw/, the beginning sound you hear in these words.

    question   **qu**iz   **qu**ack

The letters wh stand for /hw/, the beginning sound you hear in these words.

    when   **wh**at   **wh**ere

Choose a word from the box to complete each sentence. Use the hint to help you.

/ks/	/kw/	/hw/
fox	quickly	wheat
wax	quarter	wheels
experiments	question	white

1. You can ask a (/kw/) _____ and get an answer.
2. A (/kw/) _____ is worth twenty-five cents.
3. Mendel did many interesting (/ks/) _____ .
4. A (/ks/) _____ is an clever animal.
5. (/hw/) _____ is the color of one of the crayons in the box.
6. You can run (/kw/) _____ when you want to get somewhere fast.
7. Bikes have two (/hw/) _____ and one seat.
8. Some crayons are made of colored (/ks/) _____ .
9. (/hw/) _____ is a kind of grain that grows in a field.

Name _____ Date _____

COMPREHENSION

Use with textbook page 108.

"The Clever Daughter-in-Law"
Complete each sentence about "The Clever Daughter-in-Law" with a word from the box.

| fire | visit | lantern | marry | wrapped |
| wives | mother | gifts | clever | third |

Long ago in China, a rich old man told his three sons that it was time for them to

_____**1.**_____ . Two of the sons found lovely _____**2.**_____ who were

sisters. The two wives often asked their husbands' father if they could go

_____**3.**_____ their mother for a few days. The old man did not like this idea.
One day the old man said that the wives could visit their mother, but they had to bring

him two _____**4.**_____ . He told his first daughter-in-law to bring him wind

_____**5.**_____ in paper. He told the other to bring him _____**6.**_____

wrapped in paper.

The two sisters did not know what to do. They sat down and began to cry. Soon a

young farm girl saw them. She told them to go and visit their _____**7.**_____ .

She would have the gifts ready when they returned. When the sisters returned, the farm

girl gave them a paper fan and a paper _____**8.**_____ with a candle inside it.
The sisters gave the gifts to their father-in-law.

The old man invited the clever girl to meet his _____**9.**_____ son. They liked

each other and were married. Now the old man had a _____**10.**_____ new

daughter-in-law.

Use cursive writing to write the last sentence.

_____

_____

_____

_____

Unit 4   Family Ties

Name _____   Date _____

SKILLS FOR WRITING

Writing Quotations in Conversations
When you write a conversation, use **quotation marks** to show the exact words each person says.

Use a **comma** before the opening quotation marks to separate the beginning of the quote from the rest of the sentence.

    The old man said**,** "Bring me two gifts."

Use a **comma** before the final quotation marks to separate the end of the quote from the rest of the sentence.

    "Bring me two gifts**,**" said the old man.

Mark each conversation with quotation marks and a comma. Then write just the words that were said.

1. It is time for you to marry said the old man.
   _____

2. The sisters asked May we go home for a few days?
   _____

3. I can help you said the young farm girl.
   _____

4. She said I will have the gifts when you return.
   _____

5. Here is fire wrapped in paper said the farm girl.
   _____

6. How lucky I am said the old man.
   _____

7. He said Now I have a happy house and a clever new daughter-in-law.
   _____

Name _____ Date _____

SPELLING

Use after the spelling lesson.

Initial, Medial, Final Digraphs /ch/, /sh/, /th/
Say the words. Listen for /ch/. Look for the letters *ch*.

Beginning	Middle	End
children	teacher	rich
China	beaches	much
chick	benches	touch

Say the words. Listen for /sh/. Look for the letters *sh*.

Beginning	Middle	End
she	fishing	dish
shows	washer	wish
shop	dishes	wash

Say the words. Listen for /th/. Look for the letters *th*.

Beginning	Middle	End
three	father	with
third	mother	fifth
their	feathers	fourth

Write the missing letters to complete each word. Use words from the boxes.

1. ri ___ ___   tea ___ ___ er   ___ ___ ina

2. di ___ ___   fi ___ ___ ing   ___ ___ ows

3. wi ___ ___   mo ___ ___ er   ___ ___ eir

Choose a word or words from the boxes to complete each sentence. Write the missing letters.

4. Long ago in ___ ___ ina there was a ri ___ ___ old man.

5. A fa ___ ___ er had ___ ___ ree sons.

6. The sisters missed ___ ___ eir mo ___ ___ er very mu ___ ___ .

7. ___ ___ e was walking wi ___ ___ her water buffalo.

8. Parents and ___ ___ ildren often have many things in common.

9. A family tree is a chart that ___ ___ ows the people in a family.

Name _____ Date _____

VOCABULARY

Use with textbook page 111.

"Family Traits"

Key Words
experiments   generations   inherit   members   traits

Complete each sentence with a Key Word from the box.

1. _____ are members of a family in the same age group.

2. _____ are characteristics inherited from your mother and father.

3. People who belong to a group are its _____ .

4. To _____ a trait is to receive it from a parent.

5. _____ are tests scientists use to prove ideas.

Write each sentence that is true.

You may inherit your father's eye color.
You may inherit your friend's eye color.

6. _____

People in a family are family members.
A father and a son are not members of a family.

7. _____

Your grandmother and you are from the same generation.
Your grandmother and you are from different generations.

8. _____

A family trait might be brown hair.
A family trait might be green hair.

9. _____

Gregor Mendel did experiments to find out about traits.
Gregor Mendel was not interested in experiments.

10. _____

Name _____ Date _____

READING STRATEGY

Use with textbook page 111.

Reread

To **reread** means to read again.

- If you do not understand what you read at first, reread the text.
- Each time you reread the text, you learn a little more.

Reread this paragraph from page 112 in your text. Then follow the directions below.

What Are Family Traits?

Family traits are ways in which family members are alike. You may have the same color hair as your mother. You may have the same color eyes as your father. Eye color and hair color are family traits. Another family trait is how tall you are. Traits like these are passed on through families. You inherit, or get, these traits from your parents and your grandparents. You will pass on these traits to your own children.

1. Write the heading.

   _____

2. Underline the sentence that answers the question in the heading.

3. Underline the three traits that the paragraph tells about.

4. List the three traits that you underlined.

   _____
   _____
   _____

5. Some traits you have are inherited from your parents. Who else did you get your traits from?

   _____

6. When you are a grown-up, what three traits might you give to your children?

   _____
   _____
   _____

GRAMMAR

Use after the grammar lesson.

Single Possessives with Apostrophes

The **possessive** form of a noun is used to show ownership. A singular noun names only one person, place, or thing. An apostrophe (') and the letter s can be added to a singular noun to show ownership.

> The book that belongs to the girl is the girl's book.
> The animals that belong on the farm are the farm's animals.
> The home that belongs to the family is the family's home.

Underline the possessive noun in each sentence.

1. The old man's house was very beautiful.
2. The lantern's candle burned brightly.
3. The girl's gifts surprised everyone.
4. The mother's smile was big when she saw her daughters.

Read the sentences. Use a possessive noun to answer each question. The first one is done for you.

5. This house belongs to the rich man. Whose house is it?
   It is the rich man's house.

6. The lantern belongs to the girl. Whose lantern is it?
   _____

7. The fan belongs to the mother. Whose fan is it?
   _____

8. The gifts belong to the man. Whose gifts are they?
   _____

9. The road belongs to the town. Whose road is it?
   _____

104   Unit 4   Family Ties

Name _____ Date _____

GRAMMAR

Use after the grammar lesson.

Plural Possessives

The **possessive** form of a plural noun is used to show ownership. A plural noun names more than one person, place, or thing. Plural nouns usually end with the letter s. An apostrophe (') is added after the letter s in a plural noun to show ownership.

    The feathers that belong to the <u>chicks</u> are the <u>chicks'</u> feathers.
    The traits that belong to the <u>parents</u> are the <u>parents'</u> traits.

Underline the possessive noun in each sentence. Then write it on the line.

1. The flowers' petals are little. _____

2. The parents' children are all grown up. _____

3. The scientists' experiments are very interesting. _____

4. The grandparents' family was in another city. _____

5. The plants' colors are beautiful. _____

Complete each sentence using a plural possessive noun. The first one is done for you.

6. The <u>ideas</u> belong to the <u>scientists</u>. They are the __*scientists' ideas*__.

7. The <u>children</u> belong to the <u>parents</u>. They are the _____.

8. The <u>members</u> belong to the <u>clubs</u>. They are the _____.

9. The <u>roots</u> belong to the <u>plants</u>. They are the _____.

10. The <u>petals</u> belong to the <u>flowers</u>. They are the _____.

Unit 4   Family Ties

Name _____ Date _____

COMPREHENSION

Use with textbook page 116.

"Family Traits"
Complete each sentence about "Family Traits" with a word from the box.

| experiments | generation | inherit |
| traits | scientist | recessive |

A family tree shows how family members are related to one another. A family tree usually shows more than one _____1._____ of a family.

Family _____2._____ are ways in which family members are alike. Eye color, hair color, and height are some family traits you can _____3._____ from your parents and grandparents.

Sometimes children do not look like their parents. A _____4._____ named Gregor Mendel wanted to find out why. He did _____5._____ with pea plants to find out the answer.

Mendel grew generations of pea plants. He learned that the trait for the red flowers was stronger than the trait for the white flowers. He called the stronger traits dominant traits. He called the weaker traits _____6._____ traits. Mendel learned that recessive traits did not appear unless the flower had been given two recessive traits by the parent plants.

Write the sentence above that tells what Mendel learned about when recessive traits appear.

_____
_____
_____
_____

Name _____ Date _____

SPELLING PATTERNS
Use after the spelling lesson.

x, qu, wh
Complete each word with the spelling pattern in the chart.

x	qu	wh
fi __	__ __ ick	__ __ at
fo __	__ __ ack	__ __ en
bo __	__ __ ote	__ __ ere
ta __	__ __ ite	__ __ y
mi __	__ __ it	__ __ ite

Choose from the words you completed in the chart. Write the word in cursive.

1. Write the word that you use to ask about the time something happened. — __ __ en

2. Write the word that rhymes with *sit*. — __ __ it

3. Write the word that rhymes with *fax*. — ta __

4. Write the word that names an animal. — fo __

5. Write the word that is the sound a duck makes. — __ __ ack

6. Write the word that you use to ask about a place. — __ __ ere

7. Write the word that means to repair something. — fi __

8. Write the word that means a person's exact words. — __ __ ote

9. Write the word that rhymes with *white*. — __ __ ite

10. Write the word you use to find out the reason something happened. — __ __ y

Unit 4   Family Ties

Name _____ Date _____

GRAMMAR
Use with textbook page 118.

Adverbs

An **adverb** is a word that usually describes the action of a verb. An adverb usually tells *how* an action happens or *when* an action happens.

> She **gently** waved the fan.

The adverb *gently* tells <u>how</u> she waved the fan.

> The wives **soon** moved into the house.

The adverb *soon* tells <u>when</u> the wives moved into the house.

Adverbs That Tell *How*	Adverbs That Tell *When*
quickly	often
clearly	soon
happily	usually
truly	always
plainly	later
exactly	now

Underline the adverb in each sentence. Write it in cursive on the line.

1. The sisters truly missed their mother. _____

2. They often went to visit their mother. _____

3. The girl happily helped the sisters. _____

4. The old man acted quickly. _____

5. The third son and the clever girl were soon married. _____

Underline the adverb in each sentence. Then write *how* or *when* to tell what the adverb describes.

6. Twins may look exactly alike. _____

7. Children always inherit traits from their parents or grandparents. _____

8. A family tree clearly shows three generations. _____

9. Parents with brown eyes usually have children with brown eyes. _____

10. The chart plainly shows green and blue chicks. _____

108   Unit 4   Family Ties

Name _____ Date _____

VOCABULARY BUILDING

Use after the vocabulary lesson.

Homophones

Homophones are words that sound exactly alike but have different spellings and different meanings.

Homophones	Meanings	Sentences
son	male child	The third son needed a wife.
sun	the star that gives Earth heat and light	The sun shines high in the sky.
to	in the direction of	She will go to her mother's house.
two	number 2	The two sisters married the two sons.
too	also	The third son got married, too.
our	belonging to us	This is our family tree.
hour	sixty minutes	They waited for an hour.
for	intended for, meant for	This is for you.
four	number 4	I have four brothers.
fore	front	He moved to the fore of the room.

Write the correct homophone to complete each sentence. Use the chart to help you.

1. The man's first (to / two / too) _____ sons were married.

2. The old man wanted his third (son / sun) _____ to marry.

3. Those family members are not part of (hour / our) _____ generation.

4. The gifts were (fore / four / for) _____ their father-in-law.

Use a pair of homophones to complete this sentence.

5. The woman's _____ stayed too long in the hot _____ .

Unit 4   Family Ties

109

Name _____   Date _____

SKILLS FOR WRITING

Use with textbook page 119.

Writing a Personal Letter
Personal letters have fewer parts than formal letters or business letters. You can share ideas with family members or close friends in a friendly letter. You can also write a friendly letter to ask for information.

Read this friendly letter. Then answer the questions below.

January 2

Dear Aunt April,

I was so sorry that you could not come to our New Year's party. There was so much snow! You were right about not driving the long distance. We heard that the plows did not come out until late in the evening.

We did miss you at the party. Mom baked your favorite carrot cupcakes and I helped decorate them. Aunt Ellen made everyone laugh with stories about her new puppies. And, of course, cousin Fred played the piano and we all sang together. Also, I made New Year's cards with funny sayings for everyone. I will be sending yours in the mail. Please write and tell me how you spent the day.

Love,
Becky

---

1. Who is the letter addressed to and who is it from?
   _____

2. What family event does this friendly letter describe?
   _____

3. What two pieces of information about the cupcakes did Becky share?
   _____

4. What information did Becky ask for?
   _____

Name _____   Date _____

WRITING PRACTICE

Use with textbook page 120.

Write about "Family Ties"
Think about what you read in Unit 4.

Think about the problem the two sisters had. What was their problem? Who helped them solve it? How did she help? Write three or more sentences about the farm girl who was so clever. Here are some words you might want to use.

folktale	clever	daughter-in-law	father-in-law
married	lantern	wrapped	

_____
_____
_____
_____
_____

Think about families. What traits do people inherit from their parents? Are all traits inherited? Write three or more sentences telling what you learned about family traits. Here are some words you might want to use.

experiments	generation	inherit	members	related
traits	parents	dominant	recessive	

_____
_____
_____
_____
_____

Unit 4   Family Ties

Name _____ Date _____

UNIT 5   The Power of Words

INTRODUCTION: LOOKING AHEAD

Use with textbook pages 122–124.

Read this paragraph. It describes the first selection in Unit 5.

> "Early Writing" tells how the people of ancient Sumer began to write. Their type of writing is one of the oldest in the world.

Answer the following questions about this paragraph.

1. What is the title of the first selection in this unit?

   _____

2. What did the people of ancient Sumer make up?

   _____

   _____

Read this paragraph. It describes the second selection in this unit.

> Sometimes it is hard to understand another language. "The Great Minu" is a story about a man who hears a word from a different language and gets confused.

Answer the following questions about this paragraph.

3. What is the title of the second selection in this unit?

   _____

4. What does the man in the story make a mistake about?

   _____

   _____

   _____

5. Do you think this selection will be fiction or nonfiction?

   _____

Name _____   Date _____

VOCABULARY

Use with textbook page 125.

"Early Writing"

Key Words
cuneiform   grain   reeds   symbols   wedges

▲ grain

▲ reeds

▲ Cuneiform symbols are shaped like wedges.

Complete each sentence with a Key Word from the box. Use the pictures to help you.

1. Long, thin plants that grow near water are called _____.

2. _____ are signs or pictures that stand for real things.

3. Farmers in Sumer grew barley, which is a _____ that people eat.

4. The people in Sumer used a form of writing called _____.

5. Cuneiform symbols were shaped like _____, or tiny triangles.

Read each sentence. Write *True* or *False* on the line next to it. If the sentence is true, write it in cursive on the line below. If the sentence is false, make it true and write the true sentence in cursive on the line below.

6. Symbols shaped like circles are called wedges.   _____

   _____

7. Signs or pictures are symbols that stand for real things.   _____

   _____

8. Cuneiform is the name of the form of reading from Sumer.   _____

   _____

Name _____   Date _____

EXTENDING VOCABULARY

Use with textbook page 125.

Using Key Words
Here are some rules for using articles with nouns.

- Use the article *a* or *an* to talk about one general person, place, or thing.
  Use *a* or *an* before singular nouns you can count.
  Use *a* before a consonant sound. Use *an* before a vowel sound.

     a triangle   **an** article

- Do not use *a* or *an* before nouns you cannot count.

     wheat   clay

- Use *the* to talk about one or more specific persons, places, or things.

     the farmer   **the** Romans

- Do not use *a*, *an*, or *the* before names of places or languages.

     Sumer   English

Write *a*, *an*, or *the* before each noun, or leave the space blank if an article is not necessary.

1. Each symbol stands for _____ word.

2. A lot of farmers grow _____ barley.

3. The biggest wedge on that vase is the symbol for _____ sun.

4. Many of _____ Sumerians raised sheep.

5. Cuneiform is _____ ancient form of writing.

6. The people of _____ Sumer needed writing for different reasons.

Write a sentence with each word from the box. Use an article in front of each word, if needed.

> reeds   symbols   grain

7. _____

8. _____

9. _____

Name _____ Date _____

READING STRATEGY

Use with textbook page 125.

Take Notes

When reading a social studies article, you can **take notes** to help you understand the text and remember facts. Follow these instructions when you take notes as you read.

- Do not take the time to write full sentences.
- Use short forms of words, such as *TV* for *television*.
- Look at your notes after you finish reading the text.

Sometimes you can use the heading questions to organize your notes. Read the information under this heading. Then read the notes under it.

Why Did People Begin Writing?

Over five thousand years ago, people living in Sumer created the first known form of writing. What made these people begin to write?

Many Sumerians were farmers. Some farmers grew grain, such as barley, for food. Other farmers raised sheep for milk and wool. As Sumer got bigger, its people needed a way to record, or write down, facts about their products.

Heading Question	Notes
Why did people begin writing?	over five thousand years ago in Sumer
	grew grain or raised sheep
	needed a way to record facts about their products

Now try taking notes of your own. Read the paragraphs and then write the heading question and notes below it.

How Did the Sumerians Write?

The Sumerians did not have paper to write on as we do today. They wrote on clay tablets—flat pieces of clay. There was a lot of clay along the Tigris and Euphrates Rivers, where many Sumerians lived. Wet clay was soft and easy to write on. When the clay dried in the sun, it became hard and strong.

The Sumerians wrote on clay with reeds, plants that grew along the rivers. They pressed the end of a reed into the clay and made pictures and marks. The marks were shaped like wedges, or small triangles. We call these marks cuneiform.

Heading Question   **Notes**

_____   _____

_____   _____

_____   _____

Name _____ Date _____

VOCABULARY BUILDING

Use after the vocabulary lesson.

Collocations

Collocations are words that appear together and form an expression. Learning collocations can help you speak more naturally and understand commonly used expressions.

Collocation	Meaning
a long time ago	in the past
how many	what number
made up	invented, created
drew a picture	made a symbol
stood for	were a sign for
looked like	were like, had the same appearance
years ago	some years in the past

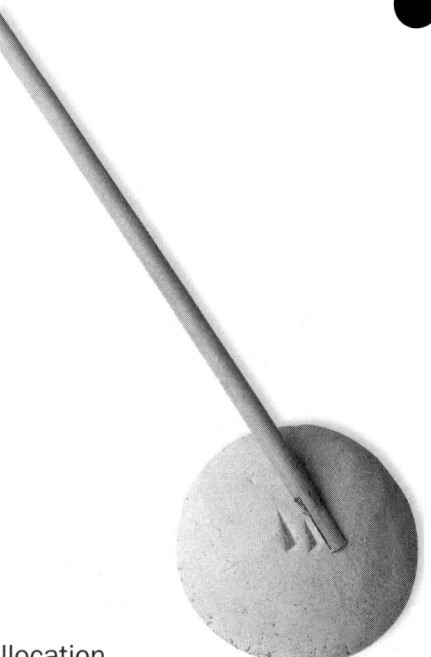

Underline the collocation in each sentence. Write the meaning of the collocation on the line below the sentence.

1. People began to write more than five thousand years ago.

   _____

2. Some people made up an early way of writing.

   _____

3. Marks stood for objects and sounds.

   _____

4. Marks that looked like sticks showed the number.

   _____

5. The sheep farmers drew a picture of a sheep.

   _____

6. Marks next to a picture showed how many sheep were sold.

   _____

7. Writing today is different from writing a long time ago.

   _____

Name _____ Date _____

PHONICS

Use after the phonics lesson.

Long Vowels: *ai, ay, eigh; ee, ea, ei*

Remember that the long vowel sound is the sound of the letter's name.

The letters *ai*, *ay*, and *eigh* often stand for the long *a* vowel sound.

    s**ai**l   s**ay**   sl**eigh**

The letters *ee*, *ea*, and *ei* often stand for the long *e* vowel sound.

    r**ee**d   r**ea**d   rec**ei**ve

Read these words with long *a* and long *e*.

Long a	Long e
clay	sheep
grain	reasons
raised	receive
way	easy
stay	read
eight	three
play	reeds

Choose the correct letters in the parentheses ( ) to complete each word in the sentences below.

1. R____ ____ds are plants that grow near water.   (*ay* or *ee*)

2. It was ____ ____sy to write with reeds.   (*ea* or *ai*)

3. Cl____ ____ was good to write on because it was soft.   (*ea* or *ay*)

4. The clay would harden and the writing would st____ ____ for a long time.   (*ay* or *ee*)

5. People needed writing for different r____ ____sons.   (*ea* or *ay*)

6. Some people r____ ____sed sheep for milk and wool.   (*ee* or *ai*)

7. The farmer wanted to know how many sh____ ____p he had sold.   (*ai* or *ee*)

8. Barley is a kind of gr____ ____n.   (*ai* or *ea*)

9. Farmers would rec____ ____ve other goods for their barley.   (*eigh* or *ei*)

10. People needed a w____ ____ to remember what they traded.   (*ei* or *ay*)

11. Three stick marks stood for the number thr____ ____.   (*ay* or *ee*)

12. Everyone learned how to r____ ____d the writing.   (*ee* or *ea*)

Unit 5   The Power of Words

Name _____   Date _____

PHONICS

Use after the phonics lesson.

Long Vowels: *oa, oe, ow; ue, ui, ew*

Remember that the long vowel sound is the sound of the letter's name.
The letters *oa, oe,* and *ow* often stand for the long *o* vowel sound.

    t**oa**d   t**oe**   t**ow**

The letters *ue, ui,* and *ew* often stand for the long *u* vowel sound.

    tr**ue**   fr**ui**t   f**ew**

Read these letters with long *o* and long *u*.

Long *o*	Long *u*
goat	cruel
hoe	suit
grown	blue
throw	duel
foe	clue
shown	drew
float	few
know	fruit

Read each word and listen for the long *o* or long *u* sound. Write two words from the chart that rhyme with each word and have the same spelling of the long vowel sound.

1. boat _____ _____

2. new _____ _____

3. row _____ _____

4. true _____ _____

5. fuel _____ _____

6. own _____ _____

7. toe _____ _____

Write two sentences. Use the word *fruit* in one and *know* in the other.

8. _____

9. _____

COMPREHENSION

Use with textbook page 130.

"Early Writing"
Complete each sentence about "Early Writing" with a word from the box.

| barley | reeds | writing | wedges | write |
| symbols | reasons | numbers | clay | larger |

Thousands of years ago, the people of Sumer made up an early way of

_____ 1. . They needed to write for different _____ 2. . For

example, a farmer might need to know how much barley he had grown. So he drew a

picture to stand for the _____ 3. . Then he added marks to show how many

acres he had harvested.

The ancient Sumerians wrote on _____ 4. . They used

_____ 5. to press marks into the soft clay. The marks were shaped like

_____ 6. . This kind of writing became known as cuneiform writing.

The _____ 7. that were used to stand for things and sounds of words

changed over time. New symbols were faster and easier to _____ 8. . The

Sumerians used marks that looked like sticks to stand for _____ 9. . These

symbols changed when the Sumerians needed to write _____ 10. numbers.

Write the last two sentences you read. Use cursive writing.

_____

_____

_____

_____

Unit 5   The Power of Words

Name _____ Date _____

SKILLS FOR WRITING

Writing Details in Outlines
You can use an outline to organize your notes. An outline has a main idea and details. Here is an outline for the text on page 126.

Main Idea
I. Reasons people began writing

Details		
1. people needed to record facts about their products	2. people had different products	3. people needed a way of remembering how much grain and how many animals they had traded

Continue the outline. Write the details from the box under the correct main ideas in the outline.

used soft clay	pressed end of a reed into clay	became simpler
stood for things	stood for sounds of words	changed to wedge-shaped
made marks	became faster and easier to write	

II. How the Sumerians wrote

    1. _____

    2. _____

    3. _____

III. What the cuneiform marks meant

    1. _____

    2. _____

IV. How the symbols changed over time

    1. _____

    2. _____

    3. _____

Name _____ Date _____

SPELLING PATTERNS

Use after the spelling lesson.

ai, ay, eigh; ee, ei, ea

Here are some spelling patterns for words with long *a*.

ai	s**ai**lor	m**ai**n
ay	w**ay**	d**ay**
eigh	w**eigh**	n**eigh**bor

Here are some spelling patterns for words with long *e*.

ee	n**ee**d	sw**ee**p
ei	c**ei**ling	**ei**ther
ea	sp**ea**k	r**ea**lly

Underline the spelling pattern for the long *a* or long *e* sound in each word. Then write the word in cursive.

Long *a* Words

1. mail _____
2. away _____
3. neighbor _____
4. grain _____
5. say _____

Long *e* Words

6. reason _____
7. sheep _____
8. receive _____
9. near _____
10. see _____

Write the word from the box that answers each question.

clay	sheep	sailor	grain	speak	rain

11. What is barley? a _____
12. Who works on a ship? a _____
13. What do you do when you talk? you _____
14. What animals are often raised on farms? _____
15. What soft material is a special kind of mud? _____
16. What makes soil on the ground wet? _____

Unit 5   The Power of Words

Name _____ Date _____

VOCABULARY

Use with textbook page 133.

"The Great Minu"

Key Words
coffin   funeral   port   sailor   village

▲ village   ▲ sailor in a port   ▲ coffin at a funeral

Complete each sentence with a Key Word from the box. Use the pictures to help you.

1. Ships come into the _____ to dock.

2. A _____ works on a ship.

3. A _____ is a small town.

4. When someone dies, people honor the person at a _____.

5. Many people walk behind the _____ during a funeral.

Write each sentence that is true.

   A port is where huge ships dock.
   A mountain is where huge ships dock.

6. _____

   Millions of people live in a village.
   Hundreds of people live in a village.

7. _____

122   Unit 5   The Power of Words

Name _____ Date _____

READING STRATEGY

Use with textbook page 133.

Understand Irony

Irony occurs in a story when the reader knows a fact about the story that a character in the story does not know at all. When you read a story, look for irony by asking yourself the following questions:

- What does a character think is the truth?
- What is really the truth?
- How does the character find out what is really going on?

Read this story and look for irony.

> Beth and Jen worked together. They ate lunch and talked each day. Every day Jen told Beth another story about Nelly.
> "Nelly and I took a long walk in the park yesterday," Jen said. "Nelly and I had such a good time."
> Beth said, "It sounds like Nelly is fun to be with."
> "Oh, she really is," said Jen.
> One day an invitation arrived.

> *Dear Jen,*
>
> *Please come to a party at my house on Saturday at 2:00. And bring your friend Nelly.*
>
> *Your friend,*
> *Beth*

> "Nelly," Jen said, as she patted her donkey. "You're invited to a party."
> Jen and Nelly arrived at the party. Beth opened the door and cried, "That's Nelly?"
> "It sure is! And you will have lots of fun with her!" said Jen.
> "More fun than I ever imagined," Beth said.

Read each question and underline the correct answer.

1. Why does Beth invite Nelly to the party?
    a. Beth thinks Nelly will bring her a gift.
    b. Beth thinks Nelly is a girl who is fun to be with.

2. What does the reader know about Nelly before the party?
    a. The reader knows that Nelly is a donkey.
    b. The reader knows that Beth is invited to a party.

3. When does Beth find out that Nelly is a donkey?
    a. Beth finds out about Nelly on the telephone.
    b. Beth finds out that Nelly is a donkey when she opens the door.

Unit 5   The Power of Words

Name _____   Date _____

GRAMMAR
Use after the grammar lesson.

Possessive Pronouns
A **possessive pronoun** is a pronoun used before a noun. A possessive pronoun is used to show ownership.

| **my** street | **its** roof | **your** home | **our** yard |
| **her** wagon | **their** houses | **his** bike | |

Underline the possessive pronoun that shows ownership in each sentence.

1. Sara will visit her friends.
2. Sara will stay at their house.
3. She will see some of our relatives, too.
4. Sara will drive her car to that town.
5. First, Sara will check its engine.
6. Is that town far from your town?

| my | your | her | his |
| its | our | their | |

Complete each sentence. Write a possessive pronoun from the box before each underlined noun.

7. I live in this house. _____ house is gray and white.
8. The house has a chimney. _____ chimney is made of red brick.
9. We have a huge garden. _____ garden is very pretty.
10. Mr. Green owns a shop. _____ shop is down the street.
11. My sister has a puppy. _____ puppy was just born.
12. My brother has a hamster. _____ hamster stays in a cage.
13. You have a little kitten. _____ kitten is very cute.
14. My friend Rick has a bike. _____ bike is brand new.
15. Lin and Nick have skates. _____ skates can go fast.
16. Sam and Jen have kites. _____ kites are yellow and green.

Name _____ Date _____

GRAMMAR

Use after the grammar lesson.

Combining Simple Sentences Using *and*

You can use the word *and* to join two **simple sentences**. Take away the period after the first sentence. Replace the part of the second sentence that repeats the first sentence with the word *and*.

 The shops were filled with rugs. The shops were filled with lamps.

 The shops were filled with rugs **and** lamps.

Circle the part of the second sentence that is repeated. Join each pair of sentences using the word *and*.

 Akwasi saw a young boy.
 Akwasi saw hundreds of cows.

1. _____

 He saw many beautiful shops.
 He saw many grand houses.

2. _____

 The houses were big.
 The houses were magnificent.

3. _____

 He thought the man owned cows.
 He thought the man owned ships.

4. _____

 Akwasi left Accra.
 Akwasi returned to his village.

5. _____

Unit 5   The Power of Words   125

Name _____   Date _____

COMPREHENSION

Use with textbook page 138.

"The Great Minu"
Write a word from the box to complete each sentence about "The Great Minu."

capital	explored	grain	gates	cows
port	sailor	village	language	houses

Akwasi lived in a small _____1._____. One day he set off for the _____2._____ city of Ghana. Akwasi walked for many days and soon came to the _____3._____ of the city. There he saw hundreds of _____4._____.
"Who owns all these cows?" Akwasi asked a boy.

The boy said, "Minu," which in the _____5._____ of Accra means "I don't understand." But Akwasi did not know the language and thought "Minu" was the name of a rich man.

As Akwasi _____6._____ the city, he came across shops and _____7._____. Each time he asked who owned them, and he was told "Minu."

Soon Akwasi came to a _____8._____ where there were many ships. He saw many bags of _____9._____. Akwasi asked a _____10._____ who owned the ships. Again he was told "Minu."

Akwasi saw a funeral procession. He asked who had died. The answer was "Minu." Akwasi thought the rich man had died, so Akwasi returned home just happy to be alive.

Write the first two sentences of the story. Use cursive writing.

_____

_____

_____

_____

Name _____ Date _____

SPELLING PATTERNS

Use after the spelling lesson.

oa, oe, ow; ue, ui, ew

Here are some spelling patterns for words with long *o*.

oa	c**oa**t	fl**oa**t
oe	t**oe**	d**oe**
ow	gl**ow**	kn**ow**

Here are some spelling patterns for words with long *u*.

ue	cl**ue**	gl**ue**
ui	j**ui**cy	cr**ui**se
ew	dr**ew**	cr**ew**

Underline the spelling pattern for the long *o* or long *u* sound in each word. Then write the word in cursive.

Long o Words

1. goat _____
2. hoe _____
3. loan _____
4. row _____
5. show _____

Long u Words

6. fruit _____
7. news _____
8. clue _____
9. suit _____
10. cruel _____

Write the word from the box next to each clue.

| new | throw | blue | float | toes | grow |

11. This is the color of the sky on a sunny day. _____
12. This is the opposite of *catch*. _____
13. Things that are just made are this. _____
14. Living plants do this. _____
15. There are five of these on a foot. _____
16. This is the opposite of *sink*. _____

Write the word that has the same spelling pattern and rhymes with each word.

17. drew _____
18. show _____
19. true _____
20. boat _____

Name _____ Date _____

GRAMMAR

Use with textbook page 140.

Pronouns

A **pronoun** is a word that takes the place of a noun.

A **subject pronoun** takes the place of a noun that is the subject of a sentence.

  subject   subject pronoun

Akwasi went to Accra. **He** went to Accra.

Subject Pronouns	
I	we
you	you
he, she, it	they

An **object pronoun** takes the place of a noun that is the object of a sentence.

  object   object pronoun

Akwasi saw **cows**. Akwasi saw **them**.

Object Pronouns	
me	us
you	you
him, her, it	them

Choose the correct pronoun to replace the underlined noun. Rewrite each sentence.

1. Akwasi said, "Akwasi will go to Accra."

   (I / Me / Him) _____

2. Accra is the capital of Ghana.

   (It / They / He) _____

3. Akwasi asked the woman a question.

   (she / he / her) _____

4. The houses were very large.

   (We / They / Them) _____

5. Akwasi saw bags on the ship.

   (they / them / we) _____

6. Molly and I liked this folktale.

   (They / You / We) _____

Name _____ Date _____

VOCABULARY BUILDING

Use after the vocabulary lesson.

Prefixes un-, re-

A **prefix** is one or more letters added to the beginning of a base word that changes the meaning of the word.

The prefix *un-* can mean *not*.

   un + happy = unhappy
   unhappy means *not happy*

The prefix *re-* can mean *again*.

   re + send = resend
   resend means *send again*

Use words from the box to complete each sentence.

unwise	rewrite
unimportant	reread
unlike	reuse

1. A man in ancient times would use symbols to show how many sheep he had. When he counted sheep again, he would _____ the same symbols.

2. Some cuneiform symbols looked like other symbols. Some cuneiform symbols were _____ other symbols.

3. It was wise of the early people of Sumer to write things down. To try to remember everything would have been _____ .

4. The people of Sumer only needed to read the symbols once to understand them. Modern researchers may need to _____ the writing many times to understand them.

5. We use the alphabet to write words. When we write something for a second time, we _____ it.

6. You might think that it is important to learn another alphabet. Or you might think it is _____ because information can be translated for you.

Unit 5   The Power of Words   129

Name _____ Date _____

SKILLS FOR WRITING
Use with textbook page 141.

Writing Notes for a Report
A **report** gives information about a topic. To write a report, first choose a topic. Then find information about that topic. One way to organize the information you find is to write notes. Write notes for each book or website you use.

Read these notes that Sam wrote. Then answer the questions.

The History of Printing
- very early printing from the ancient Chinese
- used blocks of wood to print
- printed on paper
- printed on silk
- might have used ideas from Babylonians and Sumerians

Source: National Geographic's How Things Work, by John Langone, National Geographic, Washington, D.C., 1999, p. 224.

---

1. What is the topic of Sam's report?
   _____

2. What source (book or website) did Sam use for these notes?
   _____
   _____
   _____

3. Choose three notes that Sam wrote and rewrite them.
   _____
   _____
   _____
   _____
   _____

Name _____ Date _____

WRITING PRACTICE

Use with textbook page 142.

Write about "The Power of Words"
Think about what you read in Unit 5.

What did the Sumerians use to write with? What did they use to write on? Why? Write three or more sentences about how the Sumerians wrote. Here are some words you might want to use.

| cuneiform | grain | reeds | symbols | wedges |

_____
_____
_____
_____
_____

What did Akwasi think people were saying? Why did he think so? Write three or more sentences about the mistake Akwasi made. Here are some words you might want to use.

| coffin | funeral | port | sailor | village |

_____
_____
_____
_____
_____

Name _____ Date _____

UNIT 6 Exploring the Senses

INTRODUCTION: LOOKING AHEAD

Use with textbook pages 144–146.

Here are the titles of the selections you will read. Complete the sentences below with the correct title.

> "The Blind Men and the Elephant"   "Animal Senses"

1. One selection I will read is a story about six blind men and an elephant.

   _____ is the title of the fable.

2. The next selection has many facts about how animals use their senses.

   _____ is the title of the

   nonfiction selection.

Complete each sentence with a word from the box. Use printing and cursive writing.

> elephant   senses
> *elephant   senses*

3. I see a blind man touching an elephant.

   I will learn about how each part of an _____ feels.

   I will learn about how each part of an _____ feels.

4. I see two different kinds of animals.

   I will learn about how different animals use their _____.

   I will learn about how different animals use their _____.

132   Unit 6   Exploring the Senses

VOCABULARY

Use with textbook page 147.

"The Blind Men and the Elephant"

Key Words
argue   elephant   gentle   trunk   tusks

▲ An elephant is a very large animal.

Circle the Key Word in each sentence.

1. An elephant is a large land animal with big, flat ears.
2. A gentle animal won't hurt you.
3. When people don't agree, they argue about who is right.
4. The long nose of an elephant is called a trunk.
5. Tusks are long, sharp teeth.

Write each sentence that is true.

> A gentle dog does not usually bite people.
> Gentle dogs often bite people.

6. _____

> An elephant's trunk is square.
> An elephant's trunk is long.

7. _____

> A tusk is the sharp tooth of an elephant.
> A tusk is the shell of a turtle.

8. _____

Name _____ Date _____

EXTENDING VOCABULARY

Use with textbook page 147.

Using Key Words
Read each Key Word. Then read the words that mean almost the same as the Key Word.

Key Word	Words That Mean Almost the Same
argue	disagree with another quarrel with words
elephant	biggest land animal huge gray animal with a trunk
gentle	kind to others calm behavior
trunk	long nose shaped like a tube long nose of an elephant
tusk	long, sharp tooth ivory tooth that sticks out

Read each sentence and look at the underlined word or words. Write the Key Word that means the same as the underlined word or words.

1. I took my little sister to the zoo to see the huge gray animal with a trunk.

   _____

2. The elephant looked friendly and was very calm.

   _____

3. I thought that the best part of the elephant was its long nose shaped like a tube.

   _____

4. My sister said the best part was the elephant's long, sharp tooth.

   _____

5. I didn't want to quarrel with my sister, so I took her to get some popcorn.

   _____

Name _____ Date _____

READING STRATEGY

Use with textbook page 147.

Make Inferences

To **make inferences** means to guess a story's meaning. Writers give clues about the story's meaning. These clues can be things that characters do and say. Follow these steps when you make inferences.

- Look for clues in the story.
- Think about what the characters do and say.
- Use these clues to guess the meaning of the story.

Read this text from "The Blind Men and the Elephant."

> Next, the third blind man touched one of the elephant's legs. It felt thick and rough. It was very tall. "No, you are wrong, my brothers. An elephant is not like a spear. It is not like a snake, either. It is like a large tree."

Read each sentence. Underline one inference the reader might make about the story's meaning from reading the sentence.

1. The third blind man touched one of the elephant's legs.

    a. The third blind man used his sense of taste to feel.

    b. The third blind man used his sense of touch to feel.

2. "No, you are wrong, my brothers."

    a. The third blind man thought only his idea was correct.

    b. The third blind man thought the other men had the right ideas.

3. "An elephant is not like a spear."

    a. The third blind man felt something sharp.

    b. The third blind man did not feel something sharp.

4. "It is like a large tree."

    a. The third blind man had never touched a tree.

    b. The third blind man knew that a tree felt thick and rough and tall.

Unit 6   Exploring the Senses

Name _____ Date _____

VOCABULARY BUILDING

Use after the vocabulary lesson.

Ordinal Numbers

Ordinal numbers tell the position of things that are placed in order. Ordinal numbers may be written as words or as numerals. Look at the chart.

Words	Numerals
first	1st
second	2nd
third	3rd
fourth	4th
fifth	5th
sixth	6th
seventh	7th
eighth	8th
ninth	9th
tenth	10th

Below each elephant is a word for the ordinal number that shows its place in line. Write the ordinal numeral that means the same.

first   second   third   fourth   fifth   sixth   seventh   eighth   ninth   tenth

_1st_ _____ _____ _____ _____ _____ _____ _____ _____ _____

Circle the ordinal number word that completes the sentence and write it on the line.

1. The (second / ninth) _____ elephant has its trunk raised.

2. The biggest elephant is (third / first) _____ in line.

3. The (fifth / seventh) _____ elephant has the longest tusks.

4. The smallest elephant is the (sixth / tenth) _____ elephant in line.

5. There is a person riding on the (fourth / eighth) _____ elephant.

Name _____ Date _____

PHONICS

Use after the phonics lesson.

Final -ed as /ed/, /d/, /t/; Final -s and -es as /s/, /z/

Many words end with the letters -ed. Final -ed has three different sounds.

/ed/	guid**ed**	hunt**ed**
/d/	playe**d**	tease**d**
/t/	talke**d**	maske**d**

Read each sentence and say the underlined word. Circle the word with the same final -ed sound. Then circle the sound of the ending.

		Word with Same Sound	Final Sound You Hear
1.	Six blind men <u>walked</u> up to a man leading an elephant.	played talked	/ed/ /t/
2.	The blind men <u>wanted</u> to feel the elephant.	hunted talked	/ed/ /t/
3.	They <u>asked</u> the man if they could touch the elephant.	started masked	/ed/ /t/
4.	The man was <u>pleased</u> to let them touch the elephant.	started teased	/ed/ /d/
5.	The elephant <u>stayed</u> still while the blind men touched it.	played masked	/d/ /t/
6.	Each blind man <u>decided</u> what the elephant was like.	guided talked	/ed/ /t/

Many words end with the letters -s or -es. Final -s or -es has two different sounds.

| /s/ | cat**s** |
| /z/ | tree**s** |

Write one sentence using a word from each column.

Story words that end with /s/ as in *cats*	Story words that end with /z/ as in *trees*
elephant**s**	animal**s**
flap**s**	babie**s**
group**s**	ear**s**
trunk**s**	herd**s**
tusk**s**	kind**s**

7. _____

Unit 6   Exploring the Senses

137

Name _____   Date _____

PHONICS

Use after the phonics lesson.

r-controlled Vowels

In a word that has a vowel followed by the letter *r*, the vowel stands for a different sound than its long or short sound. The letter *r* after a vowel controls the vowel's sound.

Vowels	a	e	i	o	u
r-controlled Vowels	ar	er	ir	or	ur

Complete each sentence by writing the word that has an *r*-controlled vowel.

1. Elephants are _____ land animals.
   (late / last / large)

2. A mother elephant takes care of _____ baby elephant.
   (her / hen / he)

3. A baby elephant can walk about half an hour after it is _____ .
   (body / bone / born)

4. A baby elephant stays close to its _____ .
   (me / mother / messy)

5. Elephants sleep _____ the hottest part of the day.
   (during / dune / dust)

Underline *ar, er, ir, or,* or *ur* in each word below. Then write the word in the correct column in the chart.

6. bark   brother   short   fur   turn
7. girl   water   large   bird   forget
8. first   purple   story   argue

ar	er	ir	or	ur

COMPREHENSION

Use with textbook page 152.

"The Blind Men and the Elephant"
Write a word from the box to complete each sentence in the paragraphs about "The Blind Men and the Elephant."

strange	tusk	leg	elephant	right
wall	tail	second	ear	touch

Six blind men met a man leading an _____1_____. The blind men asked to _____2_____ the elephant. The first blind man thought the elephant's sharp _____3_____ was like a spear. The _____4_____ blind man thought the elephant's long trunk was like a snake. The third blind man thought the elephant's thick _____5_____ was like a tree. The fourth blind man thought the elephant's side was like a _____6_____. The fifth blind man thought the elephant's flapping _____7_____ was like a fan. The sixth blind man thought the elephant's long, thin _____8_____ was like a rope.

Each blind man thought his idea about the elephant was _____9_____. The man with the elephant said that an elephant is something huge and _____10_____.

Write the last paragraph above. Use cursive writing.

_____

_____

_____

_____

Unit 6   Exploring the Senses

Name _____   Date _____

SKILLS FOR WRITING
Use with textbook page 153.

Poems with Rhyming Words
Read each pair of words aloud. Listen to how they rhyme.

men	then
tall	wall
care	scare
shake	snake

Read each poem. Listen for the words that rhyme. Find the missing word in the box above and write it on the line to complete the poem.

1. Six blind men
   lined up and then,
   one touched an elephant's side.
   It felt like a great big wall,
   hard and flat and _____ .

2. One man touched the trunk with care.
   It began to shake.
   It gave the man a terrible scare.
   He thought he held a _____ !

3. Use cursive writing to copy one of the poems above.

   _____
   _____
   _____
   _____
   _____

4. Circle the illustration that is about the poem you copied. Then circle the rhyming words in the poem.

Name _____ Date _____

SPELLING

Use after the spelling lesson.

Adding -ing, -ed, -s, and -es to Base Words
The endings -ing and -ed can be added to base words.

    walk   walk**ing**   walk**ed**

Remember the 1–1–1 rule: When a word of *one syllable* has *one vowel* and ends in *one consonant*, double the final consonant before adding -ing or -ed.

    stop   stop**ping**   stop**ped**

Add -ing and -ed to each base word and write the new words.

1. look _____ _____
2. jump _____ _____
3. start _____ _____
4. turn _____ _____

Use the 1–1–1 rule. Double the final consonant of each base word, then add -ing and -ed.

5. tap _____ _____
6. drop _____ _____
7. skip _____ _____
8. scrub _____ _____

Add -s to a noun to make it mean more than one.

    elephant**s**   tusk**s**

Add -es to a noun that ends in x, s, z, ch, or sh to make it mean more than one.

    wish**es**   bunch**es**

Add -s or -es to make the noun mean more than one. Write the new word.

9. bus _____   12. bird _____
10. sandwich _____   13. fox _____
11. cup _____   14. frog _____

Unit 6   Exploring the Senses

Name _____ Date _____

VOCABULARY

Use with textbook page 155.

"Animal Senses"

Key Words
hive   predators   prey   survive   vision

▲ The owl is the predator and the mouse is its prey.

Underline the Key Word in each sentence.

1. If you have good vision, it means you can see well.
2. A hive is a place where bees make their home and honey is made.
3. To survive means to stay alive.
4. Animals that are predators catch and eat other animals.
5. Animals that are prey are often eaten by other animals.

Write each sentence that is true.

The owl with good vision could see the little frog.
The owl with good vision could not see the little frog.

6. _____

Honeybees flew home to the den.
Honeybees flew home to the hive.

7. _____

The lion was a predator, so he caught and ate the deer.
The lion was a predator, so he caught and ate some leaves.

8. _____

Name _____ Date _____

READING STRATEGY

Use with textbook page 155.

Find Main Ideas

The **main ideas** are the most important ideas in the text. Each paragraph usually has one main idea. Finding main ideas as you read can help you remember the important parts of the text. Follow these steps as you look for the main ideas.

- Use headings and words in dark type as clues to main ideas.
- Remember that the first sentence of a paragraph often tells the main idea.
- Look for facts that support the main idea in each paragraph.

Read this information about elephants' trunks.

> Elephants also touch each other with their trunks to communicate. Friendly elephants touch trunks as a greeting. Mother elephants touch new baby elephants with their trunks to welcome them. When a baby elephant is afraid, the mother strokes it with her trunk. Sometimes a baby elephant holds its mother's tail with its trunk. That makes the baby feel safe.

Underline the first sentence. It tells the main idea. Write the main idea of this paragraph.

1. _____

Write *Fact* on the line if the sentence tells a fact that supports the main idea.

2. _____ Elephants have small eyes.
3. _____ Friendly elephants touch trunks as a greeting.
4. _____ Elephants use their sense of hearing to avoid danger.
5. _____ Sometimes a baby elephant holds its mother's tail with its trunk.
6. _____ Owls have excellent vision.
7. _____ Elephants cannot see well.
8. _____ Elephants use their sense of hearing to avoid danger.
9. _____ When a baby elephant is afraid, the mother strokes it with her trunk.
10. _____ Mother elephants touch new baby elephants with their trunks to welcome them.

Unit 6   Exploring the Senses

Name _____   Date _____

GRAMMAR

Use after the grammar lesson.

Prepositions

Prepositions are words that tell *where,* *in what direction,* or *when.*

under	up	after	in	across
to	at	on	down	before

Underline the preposition in each sentence.

1. The dog is under the table.
2. My friend lives across the street.
3. We will go down the hill.
4. Juan is at my house.
5. I will come on Monday.
6. He walked to the door.
7. I rode my bike up the road.
8. I will go home after school.
9. There is a fly in this room.
10. I look before I start.

Read each sentence about an elephant. Underline the question that is answered by the preposition in the sentence.

11. An elephant walked <u>up</u> the hill.   where?   when?   in what direction?
12. A bird sat <u>on</u> the elephant.   where?   when?   in what direction?
13. The elephant stopped <u>under</u> a tree.   where?   when?   in what direction?
14. The elephant rested <u>after</u> a meal.   where?   when?   in what direction?

144   Unit 6   Exploring the Senses

Name _____ Date _____

GRAMMAR

Use after the grammar lesson.

Combining Simple Sentences Using *but*
You can join two sentences using the word *but*. Change the period after the first sentence to a comma and make the capital letter that begins the second sentence lowercase.

> Jen knew a lot about elephants. She learned two new facts.
> Jen knew a lot about elephants**,** **but** she learned two new facts.

Join each pair of sentences using the word *but*.

1. Most animals have five senses.
   They use one or two more important senses to survive.

   _____
   _____

2. Elephants cannot see well.
   They have a good sense of smell.

   _____
   _____

3. Elephants may not see rain that is far away.
   They know where to find rainwater.

   _____
   _____

4. Most birds cannot see well at night.
   Owls can see well in the dark.

   _____
   _____

5. Honeybees cannot hear well.
   They have a good sense of touch.

   _____
   _____

Unit 6   Exploring the Senses

COMPREHENSION

Use with textbook page 160.

"Animal Senses"
Write a word from the box to complete each sentence in the paragraphs below.

survive	trunk	important	ground	night
dance	hunting	touch	water	prey

Animals use their senses to _____1._____ in nature. Their abilities to see, hear, taste, smell, and _____2._____ help them to find food. Sometimes one or two senses are more _____3._____ for an animal than the others.

An elephant mostly uses its senses of smell and touch to find food and _____4._____. An elephant smells with its _____5._____. An elephant's feet can feel vibrations in the _____6._____. The vibrations help the elephant know where to find rainwater.

An owl can see very well and uses that sense when _____7._____ for food. An owl can see well at _____8._____. It finds its _____9._____ in the dark.

Honeybees mostly use their senses of touch and smell. Honeybees _____10._____ in a circle to tell other bees where to find food and nectar.

Write the sentences that tell about honeybees. Use cursive writing.

_____

_____

_____

_____

_____

146   Unit 6   Exploring the Senses

Name _____ Date _____

SPELLING PATTERNS

Use after the spelling lesson.

ar, er, ir, or, ur
Complete each word with the spelling pattern that begins the row.

1. ar   h___ ___d   sh___ ___p   l___ ___ge
2. er   wat___ ___   read___ ___   moth___ ___
3. ir   th___ ___d   f___ ___st   s___ ___
4. or   f___ ___   st___ ___y   b___ ___n
5. ur   h___ ___t   t___ ___n   b___ ___n

Choose from the words you completed above. Write the word in cursive.

6. Write the word that is the place before second.   ___*ir*___ ___
7. Write the word that is the place after second.   ___ ___*i*___
8. Write the word that rhymes with *burn*.   ___*ur*___
9. Write the word that means a liquid you drink.   ___ ___ ___*er*
10. Write the word that means the opposite of *small*. ___*ar*___ ___
11. Write the word that begins with *st*.   ___ ___*or*___
12. Write the word that begins with *sh*.   ___ ___*ar*___
13. Write the word that rhymes with *brother*.   ___ ___ ___ ___*er*

Unit 6   Exploring the Senses

Name _____ Date _____

GRAMMAR

Use after the grammar lesson.

Prepositional Phrases

A **prepositional phrase** begins with a preposition and ends with a noun or pronoun.

A **preposition** is a word that tells *where*, *in what direction*, or *when*.

A **noun** is a word that names a person, place, or thing.

Prepositions		Nouns	
on	after	car	school
under	into	hill	tree
before	to	table	rain
from	up	house	road

Underline the preposition in each of the prepositional phrases below. Then circle the noun in each phrase.

1. to the car
2. after the rain
3. under the tree
4. before school
5. on the table
6. up the hill

Write a preposition and a noun from the chart above to complete each sentence. You may use the words more than one time.

7. I went home _____ _____.
8. The cat climbed _____ the _____.
9. The ball rolled _____ the _____.
10. It was cloudy _____ the _____.
11. A leaf fell _____ the _____.
12. A girl slowly walked _____ the _____.
13. A dog ran _____ the _____.
14. A boy skated _____ the _____.
15. My mom went _____ the _____.

Circle the prepositional phrase in each sentence above.

Name _____   Date _____

VOCABULARY BUILDING

Use after the vocabulary lesson.

Homographs

A **homograph** is a word that is spelled exactly like another word but has a different meaning.

Homographs	Meaning	
second	comes after first	part of a minute
cried	yelled	shed tears
trunk	long nose of an elephant	large box to keep things in
right	correct	a direction
blind	unable to see	window shade

Read each sentence and find the underlined word. Write the correct meaning of the word. Use the chart to help you.

1. Wait just a second. _____

2. "I won! I won!" she cried. _____

3. We can store the clothes in a trunk. _____

4. I am wrong and you are right. _____

5. Pull down the blind to keep out the sun. _____

6. Who is the second person in line? _____

Unit 6   Exploring the Senses

Name _____   Date _____

SKILLS FOR WRITING

Use with textbook page 163.

Writing a Descriptive Paragraph

A **description** is a piece of writing that tells what something is like. A writer uses sensory words to tell what it is like to see, hear, touch, taste, or smell something. Writers use adjectives to help the reader picture what is being described.

Read this description of a guinea pig. Then answer the questions.

> I recently got a guinea pig for a birthday present. This guinea pig is a very cute animal. I named her Ruby, for her red eyes. She is small and round and covered with soft white fur. She gets really excited when she knows I am about to feed her. She stands up on her hind legs and makes a long, loud squeal. She has long, sharp front teeth. When I give her a piece of lettuce, she nibbles on it quickly. I think she is often thirsty. She drinks a lot of water from her water bottle.
>
> I am really happy to have Ruby as my pet. I think I will go and feed her right now!

1. Write the sentence that describes what the guinea pig's eyes look like.

   _____

2. Write the two adjectives that describe the guinea pig's size and shape.

   _____   _____

3. Write the adjective that describes how the guinea pig's fur feels.

   _____

4. Write the two adjectives that describe the guinea pig's squeal.

   _____   _____

5. Write the sentence that describes the guinea pig's front teeth.

   _____

6. Write the sentence that describes how the writer feels about having Ruby for a pet.

   _____

Name _____ Date _____

WRITING PRACTICE

Use with textbook page 164.

Write about "Exploring the Senses"
Think about what you read in Unit 6.

In "The Blind Men and the Elephant," each man had a different idea of what an elephant is like. How would you describe an elephant? Write three sentences that you think best describe an elephant. Here are some words you may want to use.

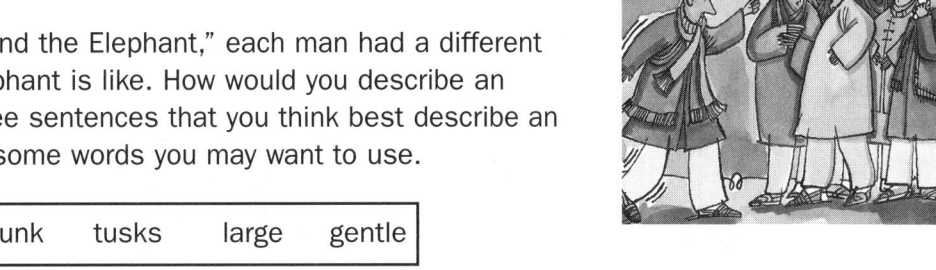

| trunk   tusks   large   gentle |

_____
_____
_____
_____
_____
_____

Think about what you learned from reading "Animal Senses." Do animals use all of their senses to get food, or do they mostly use one or two? Write three sentences about which sense owls mostly use and how it helps them. Here are some words you may want to use.

| vision   night   front   predator   prey |
| mice   rabbits rabbits frogs   bird |

_____
_____
_____
_____
_____
_____

Unit 6   Exploring the Senses

Name _____ Date _____

UNIT 7 The World of Plants

INTRODUCTION: LOOKING AHEAD

Use with textbook pages 166–168.

Here are some pictures from Unit 7.

▲ A flower is part of a plant. I will learn about different parts of plants.

▲ A bird is near the flower. I will find out how birds help plants.

Remember, the title of Unit 7 is "The World of Plants." Circle the things you think you will read about in this unit.

    flowers   fruit   leaves   cars   computers   seeds   stems

Write four of the words you circled on the lines below. First print the word, then write it in cursive writing.

1. _____ _____

2. _____ _____

3. _____ _____

4. _____ _____

Here are the titles of the selections you will read. Complete each sentence with the correct title.

| "Amazing Plants"   "Apollo and Daphne" |

5. _____ is the title of the myth I will read.

6. _____ is the title of the nonfiction selection I will read.

152   Unit 7   The World of Plants

VOCABULARY

Use with textbook page 169.

"Amazing Plants"

Key Words			
absorb	oxygen	pollen	pollination
release	reproduce	roots	stem

▲ A plant's roots absorb water.

▲ Pollen is used in the pollination of plants.

▲ Some plants have very long stems.

Complete each sentence with a Key Word from the box. Use the pictures to help you.

1. To _____ means to make offspring.

2. _____ is a gas in the air that has no smell, taste, or color.

3. A sponge can be used to _____ water.

4. _____ is necessary for plants to make seeds for new plants.

5. The _____ of a plant take in water and minerals from the ground.

6. Flowers make a yellow powder called _____ .

7. The _____ is the main part of a plant that holds up the leaves and flowers.

8. Trees and plants _____ oxygen into the air we breathe.

Write each sentence that is true.

Plants reproduce when sunlight hits them.
Plants reproduce when they form seeds.

9. _____

Tree roots take in water from the ground.
Tree roots take in water from the air.

10. _____

Unit 7   The World of Plants

Name _____ Date _____

EXTENDING VOCABULARY

Use with textbook page 169.

Using Key Words
Read each Key Word. Then read the words that mean almost the same as the Key Word.

Key Words	Words That Mean Almost the Same
absorb	take in; soak up
oxygen	an invisible, odorless gas; one of the gases in the air
pollen	yellowish powder produced by a flower; powder that plants use in reproduction
pollination	moving pollen from one flower to another
release	give off
reproduce	make offspring
roots	underground parts of a plant
stem	main stalk

Read each sentence and look at the underlined words. Write the Key Word that means the same as the underlined words.

1. In science class, we learned that plants make an invisible, odorless gas. _____

2. The teacher showed us a plant that had a flower with powder that plants use in reproduction on it. _____

3. He told us that insects, birds, and other animals help plants by performing the process of moving pollen from one flower to another. _____

4. The teacher said that flowers use pollen to form seeds to make offspring. _____

5. Next he showed us the plant's main stalk. _____

6. Finally, he showed us the plant's underground parts. _____

7. He told us that the roots soak up water from the ground. _____

8. Plants help us live because they give off oxygen into the air. _____

Name _____ Date _____

READING STRATEGY

Use with textbook page 169.

Use Diagrams
Use **diagrams** in a science text to give you important information. Follow these steps as you study a diagram.

- Look at the diagram carefully.
- Read all the labels.
- Think about the ideas in the text that each diagram makes clearer.

Read this caption from your textbook. Use the words in dark type to label the diagram.

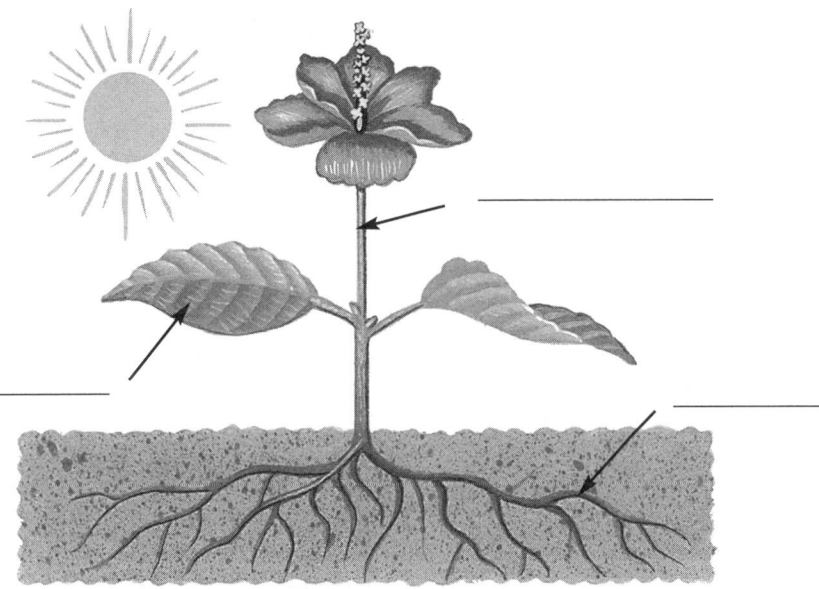

▲ The **roots** of a plant absorb, or take in, water from the ground. The **stem** holds up the plant. The **leaves** absorb sunlight and release, or give off, oxygen, an important gas.

Read each sentence. Write *True* or *False*.

1. A diagram may give information that is not in the text. _____

2. This diagram shows the color of the plant parts. _____

3. This diagram shows many different plants. _____

4. This diagram shows what this plant's parts look like. _____

5. This diagram shows where this plant's parts are located. _____

6. This diagram shows a fruit. _____

Unit 7   The World of Plants   155

Name _____ Date _____

VOCABULARY BUILDING

Use after the vocabulary lesson.

Regular Comparatives with -er and -est

Comparative adjectives end with the suffix *-er* and compare two or more things.

Superlative adjectives end with the suffix *-est* and compare three or more things.

Adjective	Comparative	Superlative
sweet	sweet**er**	sweet**est**
red	redd**er**	redd**est**
tall	tall**er**	tall**est**
small	small**er**	small**est**
big	bigg**er**	bigg**est**

tall   taller   tallest

Choose the correct form of the word in parentheses and write it in the sentence. Use the chart to help.

1. Cherries taste (sweet / sweeter / sweetest) _____ .

2. The beets I planted are the (small / smaller / smallest) _____ beets of all.

3. Jesse's plant is (small / smaller / smallest) _____ than Un's plant.

4. Of all the corn the boys planted, Jin's corn is the (tall / taller / tallest) _____ .

5. Luis's tomato was the (red / redder / reddest) _____ tomato in the garden.

6. Some apples are (red / redder / reddest) _____ .

7. Peaches are (sweet / sweeter / sweetest) _____ than lemons.

8. The grapes are (big / bigger / biggest) _____ than the cherries.

9. That is the (sweet / sweeter / sweetest) _____ strawberry of all.

10. Watermelons are the (big / bigger / biggest) _____ fruit that we planted.

Name _____ Date _____

PHONICS

Use after the phonics lesson.

Final and Medial -tion

The letters -tion stand for /shun/ at the end of these words:

    na**tion**   constitu**tion**   sta**tion**

The letters -tion stand for /shun/ in the middle of these words:

    na**tion**al   constitu**tion**al   sta**tion**ary

Say these words aloud. Circle *middle* or *end* to tell where you hear the /shun/ sound.

1. pollina**tion**   middle   end
2. na**tion**al   middle   end
3. ques**tion**   middle   end
4. cap**tion**   middle   end
5. dic**tion**ary   middle   end
6. sta**tion**ary   middle   end
7. emo**tion**al   middle   end
8. informa**tion**   middle   end
9. nonfic**tion**   middle   end
10. defini**tion**   middle   end

Use a word with -tion from above to complete each sentence below.

11. Fiction is a story, but _____ is true.

12. A _____ tells information about a picture.

13. I find the meaning of words in a _____ .

14. I can find out the meaning of a word by reading its _____ .

15. I know that _____ is when an insect or animal moves pollen to another flower.

16. There is so much _____ about plants in this unit.

17. Now I can answer every _____ about the article.

Unit 7   The World of Plants

Name _____ Date _____

PHONICS

Use after the phonics lesson.

Diphthongs: ow, ou; oi, oy; aw, au

Diphthongs are vowel sounds that combine two sounds and are spelled with two letters.

The letters *ow* and *ou* stand for the sound you hear at the end of *now*.

    h**ow**   c**ow**   gr**ou**nd   f**ou**nd

The letters *oi* and *oy* stand for the sound you hear at the end of *boy*.

    b**oi**l   n**oi**se   t**oy**   j**oy**

The letters *aw* and *au* stand for the sound you hear at the end of *draw*.

    s**aw**   p**aw**   t**au**ght   c**au**ght

Think about the sound the underlined letters stand for in each word. Write each word under the correct heading in the chart below.

enj*oy*   *aw*ful   v*oi*ce   p*ow*er   r*ou*nd   fl*ow*er
f*ou*nd   *Au*gust   *oi*l   c*au*ght   *aw*esome   s*oy*

ow and **ou** as in **now**	**oi** and **oy** as in **boy**	**aw** and **au** as in **draw**
1.	5.	9.
2.	6.	10.
3.	7.	11.
4.	8.	12.

Find and write the two words in each sentence that have the same diphthong.

13. Now I can see the new flower blooming.

    _____   _____

14. I found a tiny, round seed inside the fruit.

    _____   _____

158   Unit 7   The World of Plants

Name _____ Date _____

COMPREHENSION

Use with textbook page 174.

"Amazing Plants"

Write a word from the box to complete each sentence about "Amazing Plants."

| breathe | photosynthesis | oxygen | ovary | ground |
| fruits | leaves | pollen | pollination | seeds |

One reason we need plants is that they give us food. We eat many kinds of foods from plants, such as grains, vegetables, _____(1)_____, and nuts. A second reason we need plants is that they release _____(2)_____ into the air. We need to take in oxygen every time we _____(3)_____.

Plants make their own food by a process called _____(4)_____. Sunlight combines with water, gases, and minerals in the _____(5)_____ of the plant.

Insects, birds, and other animals help plants by carrying _____(6)_____ from one flower to another. This process is called _____(7)_____. After pollination, the _____(8)_____ in the center of the flower grows larger. It becomes a fruit with _____(9)_____ inside. When the seeds fall to the _____(10)_____, a new cycle of plant life begins.

Write the paragraph that tells two reasons why we need plants. Use cursive writing.

_____
_____
_____
_____
_____
_____
_____

Unit 7   The World of Plants

SKILLS FOR WRITING

Writing Similes

A **simile** is a way of comparing two things. In a simile, you use the word *like*.

▲ An orange is round, **like** a basketball.　　▲ Donna's cheeks are **like** red apples.

The simile compares an orange to a basketball.　　The simile compares cheeks to apples.

Write the two things that are being compared in each sentence.

1. A mushroom is like an umbrella.　　_____ _____
2. A plant's stem is like a straw.　　_____ _____
3. Wan is tall, like a cornstalk.　　_____ _____
4. A tomato is red, like a stop sign.　　_____ _____
5. A cucumber is like a baseball bat.　　_____ _____

Write a simile for each pair of things. Use the word *like* to compare them. Use cursive writing.

　　lemon　　sun

6. _____

　　melon　　soccer ball

7. _____

　　leaves　　grass

8. _____

Name _____ Date _____

SPELLING

Use after the spelling lesson.

Diphthongs: *ow, ou; oi, oy; aw, au*
Diphthongs are vowel sounds that combine two sounds and are spelled with two letters.

The letters *ow* and *ou* stand for the sound you hear at the end of *now*.

    t**ow**n   pl**ow**   s**ou**nd   r**ou**nd

The letters *oi* and *oy* stand for the sound you hear at the end of *boy*.

    s**oi**l   ch**oi**ce   enj**oy**   s**oy**

The letters *aw* and *au* stand for the sound you hear at the end of *draw*.

    l**aw**   cl**aw**   **Au**gust   c**au**ght

Read the words in the box.

brown	toy	found	hawk	coin	cause
taught	broil	how	joy	pound	straw

Write the four words that have the same sound you hear at the end of *now*.
Circle the letters that stand for the sound.

1. _____   3. _____

2. _____   4. _____

Write the four words that have the same sound you hear at the end of *boy*.
Circle the letters that stand for the sound.

5. _____   7. _____

6. _____   8. _____

Write the four words that have the same sound you hear at the end of *draw*.
Circle the letters that stand for the sound.

9. _____   11. _____

10. _____   12. _____

Write a rhyming word next to each word.

13. law _____   14. oil _____

Unit 7   The World of Plants

VOCABULARY

Use with textbook page 177.

"Apollo and Daphne"

Key Words
arrows   bark   bow   crowns   forest

▲ a bow and arrow

▲ The trees in the forest are covered with bark.

Complete each sentence with a Key Word from the box. Use the pictures to help you.

1. Kings and queens wear _____ on their heads.

2. A _____ is a curved piece of wood that is used to shoot arrows.

3. Trees are covered with _____ .

4. _____ are long pointed sticks that can be shot from bows.

5. Many trees and plants grow in the _____ .

Read each sentence. Write *True* or *False* on the line next to it. If the sentence is true, write it in cursive on the line below. If the sentence is false, make it true and write the true sentence in cursive on the line below.

6. You can wear a crown on your head. _____

_____

7. There are few trees in a forest. _____

_____

8. Bark is on the outside of trees. _____

_____

9. You use a bow to plant flowers. _____

_____

Name _____ Date _____

READING STRATEGY

Use with textbook page 177.

Visualize

To **visualize** means to picture something in your mind. Follow these steps as you complete this page.

- As you read, look for words that describe the characters.
- Look for details that tell when and where the characters lived.
- Look for words that describe their actions.

1. Read the sentence. Underline the words that describe Cupid.

    One day Cupid, the young god of love, was playing with his bow and arrows.

2. Read the sentence. Underline the words that describe Apollo.

    Cupid wanted to be a great hunter like his uncle, Apollo.

3. Read the two sentences. Underline the words that describe each character's actions.

    Cupid shot one of his arrows at Apollo. Apollo laughed.

Use the words you underlined to help you picture Cupid and Apollo in your mind.

4. Use these words from the text on page 179 to help you picture Daphne.

    | very beautiful | long hair | fair skin | very shy |

Write a description of how you picture Daphne. Use cursive writing.

_____
_____
_____
_____
_____

Unit 7   The World of Plants

Name _____ Date _____

GRAMMAR

Use after the grammar lesson.

Positive and Negative Sentences

A **positive sentence** tells what something is, has, or does.

A **negative sentence** tells what something is not, does not have, or does not do. Negative sentences often use the word *not*.

Write *P* for *positive* or *N* for *negative* next to each sentence.

1. _____ Cupid follows his uncle everywhere.

2. _____ The arrow does not hurt Apollo.

3. _____ Daphne is afraid and runs away.

4. _____ Daphne did not stop.

5. _____ She is now a beautiful laurel tree.

Use the word *not* to rewrite these positive sentences as negative ones. Write in cursive.

6. Cupid was playing with his kite.
   _____

7. Cupid is the son of Apollo.
   _____

8. Venus is the goddess of flowers.
   _____

9. Apollo did know the power of Cupid's arrows.
   _____

10. He did know that he was going to fall in love.
    _____

164   Unit 7   The World of Plants

GRAMMAR

Use after the grammar lesson.

Sentences with Compound Subjects

The **subject** of a sentence is the person or thing that is doing or being something.

Read each sentence. Underline *who* or *what* is doing or being something.

1. Venus is the goddess of love and beauty.
2. Cupid was playing with his bow and arrows.
3. Daphne ran away quickly.

Sentences have **compound subjects** when two or more people or things are doing or being something. The two subjects are joined by the word *and*.

Read each sentence. Write the two subjects in each sentence.

4. Apollo and Cupid are gods. _____ _____
5. Daphne and Apollo ran in the forest. _____ _____
6. Peaches and apples are fruits. _____ _____
7. Stems and leaves can be green. _____ _____
8. Insects and birds are animals. _____ _____
9. Carrots and potatoes are vegetables. _____ _____

Write three sentences from above. Use cursive writing.

_____
_____
_____

Unit 7   The World of Plants

Name _____ Date _____

COMPREHENSION

Use with textbook page 182.

"Apollo and Daphne"
Write a word from the box to complete each sentence about "Apollo and Daphne."

small	laurel	laughed	angry	afraid
river	love	Daphne	crown	arrows

Venus, the goddess of love and beauty, gave some _____**1.**_____ to Cupid. The arrows were special and caused people to fall in _____**2.**_____. Cupid wanted to be a great hunter like Apollo, his uncle. Apollo told Cupid he was too _____**3.**_____ to be a hunter. This made Cupid very _____**4.**_____, and he shot one of his arrows at Apollo. Apollo _____**5.**_____ because he did not know the power of Cupid's arrows.

Apollo saw a forest nymph named _____**6.**_____. When Apollo tried to go near Daphne, she was _____**7.**_____ and ran away. Daphne called out to her father, the _____**8.**_____ god, to help her. The river god changed Daphne into a _____**9.**_____ tree. Apollo wore a _____**10.**_____ of laurel leaves in honor of Daphne.

Write the last two sentences of the story. Use cursive writing.

_____
_____
_____
_____

Name _____ Date _____

SPELLING PATTERNS

Use after the spelling lesson.

Final -*tion*, -*sion*

Some words end with the letters -*tion* or -*sion*.

Complete each word with the spelling patterns in the box.

-tion	-sion
pollina _t_ _i_ _o_ _n_	vi __ __ __ __
cap __ __ __ __	televi __ __ __ __
frac __ __ __ __	man __ __ __ __
reproduc __ __ __ __	explo __ __ __ __

Use the words you wrote. Complete each word below.

1. Write the word that starts with the letters *re* and means a plant making new plants.

   __ __ __ __ __ __ __ __tion

2. Write the math word that means part of a number.

   __ __ __ __tion

3. Write the word that means a big, grand house.

   __ __ __sion

4. Write the word that begins with the letters *ex*.

   __ __ __ __ __sion

5. Write the word that describes a bee carrying pollen from one flower to another.

   __ __ __ __ __ __ __tion

6. Write the word that is something you might watch to see your favorite show.

   __ __ __ __ __ __sion

7. Write the word that describes the words that appear under a photo.

   __ __ __tion

8. Write the word that is another word for *sight*.

   __ __sion

Unit 7   The World of Plants

Name _____ Date _____

GRAMMAR

Use after textbook page 184.

Comparison with Adjectives

Use an **adjective** to describe or modify **one thing**.

Use **comparative adjectives** to compare **two or more things**.

Use **superlative adjectives** to compare **three or more things**.

For these adjectives, add *-er* for comparatives and *-est* for superlatives

Adjective	Comparative	Superlative
tall	tall**er than**	**the** tall**est**
cold	cold**er than**	**the** cold**est**
easy	eas**ier than**	**the** eas**iest**

Write the correct adjective form on the line. Use the chart to help you. Look for the clue words *than* and *the*.

1. December is usually (cold / colder / coldest) _____ than May.

2. The math test was (easy / easier / easiest) _____ .

3. Sue is (tall / taller / tallest) _____ than Tia.

4. Washing dishes is the (easy / easier / easiest) _____ chore of all.

For these adjectives, keep the same spelling and use *more* for comparatives and *most* for superlatives.

Adjective	Comparative	Superlative
beautiful	**more** beautiful **than**	**the most** beautiful
colorful	**more** colorful **than**	**the most** colorful

Write the correct adjective form on the line. Use the chart to help you. Look for the clue words *than* and *the*.

5. Sara's dress is (colorful / more colorful / most colorful) _____ than Jan's.

6. Jane has the (beautiful / more beautiful / most beautiful) _____ eyes of any girl I know.

7. That rose is (beautiful / more beautiful / most beautiful) _____ .

8. Marty had the (colorful / more colorful / most colorful) _____ kite.

Name _____ Date _____

VOCABULARY BUILDING

Use after the vocabulary lesson.

Irregular Comparatives and Superlatives
These adjectives have **irregular comparative** and **superlative** forms.

Adjective (one thing)	Comparative (two or more things)	Superlative (three or more things)
good	better **than**	**the** best
bad	worse **than**	**the** worst
much	more **than**	**the** most
little	less **than**	**the** least

Choose the adjective to describe one thing, the comparative to compare two or more things, or the superlative to compare three or more things. Look for the clue words *than* and *the*.

1. James got the (bad / worse / worst) _____ grade in the class.

2. Miguel has (much / more / most) _____ trophies than Ryan or Jane.

3. Tim had a (bad / worse / worst) _____ score than Rachel.

4. Cindy has a (bad / worse / worst) _____ cold.

5. The children were (good / better / best) _____ while their mother was busy.

6. Pete has the (much / more / most) _____ marbles of the three boys.

7. I have a (little / less / least) _____ juice in my cup.

8. Mom's cookies are (good / better / best) _____ than her chocolate cake.

9. Steve has (little / less / least) _____ homework than Kyle or Lucy.

10. My cat eats the (little / less / least) _____ of all the cats on our block.

Unit 7   The World of Plants

Name _____ Date _____

SKILLS FOR WRITING

Use with textbook page 185.

Writing a Comparison

A **comparison** tells how two people, places, or things are alike and different.

Read this comparison. The writer uses the word *both* to show how the things are alike. The writer uses comparative forms of adjectives to show how they are different. Then answer the questions below.

Two Wonderful Fruits

A lemon and a peach are alike in many ways. A lemon and a peach are both fruits that grow on trees. Both fruits protect their seeds. Both fruits are juicy.

A lemon and a peach are different in many ways. A lemon has an oval shape, while a peach is round. A lemon has a tougher outer skin than a peach. A peach tastes much sweeter than a lemon. A lemon has many seeds, but a peach has only one.

1. What two things did the writer compare?

   _____   _____

2. What is the first paragraph mostly about?

   _____

3. What is one way a lemon and a peach are alike?

   _____

4. What is the second paragraph mostly about?

   _____

5. Which two comparative adjectives did the writer use?

   _____   _____

Name _____ Date _____

WRITING PRACTICE
Use with textbook page 186.

Write about "Amazing Plants"
Think about what you read in Unit 7.

What amazing facts did you learn about plants? Write three or four sentences that tell how plants make their own food or how they reproduce. Use cursive writing. Here are some words you may want to use.

| absorb | oxygen | pollen | pollination |
| release | reproduce | roots | stem |

_____
_____
_____
_____
_____

What do laurel leaves stand for? Write three or more sentences about a boy or girl who wins a trophy decorated with a crown of laurel leaves. Use cursive writing.

_____
_____
_____
_____
_____

Unit 7 The World of Plants

UNIT 8 Wings

INTRODUCTION: LOOKING AHEAD

Use with textbook pages 188–190.

Read this paragraph. It tells about the first two selections in Unit 8.

> In Part 1, you will learn about Bessie Coleman, a woman who dreamed of flying and made her dream come true. Then you will read a poem about dreams and flying.

Answer the following questions about this paragraph.

1. What is the name of the person you will learn about in Part 1?

   _____

2. What did Bessie Coleman dream of doing?

   _____

3. What will be the subject of the poem in Part 1?

   _____

Read this paragraph. It describes the selections in Part 2 of the unit.

> In Part 2, you will read a story about a boy who rescues a pigeon with a broken wing. Finally, you will read about a bird that saved the lives of American soldiers.

Answer the following questions.

4. What is wrong with the pigeon that the boy rescues in the first story in Part 2?

   _____

5. In the second selection in this part, whose lives did the bird save?

   _____

172 Unit 8 Wings

Name _____ Date _____

VOCABULARY

Use with textbook page 191.

"Bessie Coleman, American Flyer"

Key Words	
encouraged	famous
publisher	thrilling
toured	

▲ a thrilling ride

Complete each sentence with a Key Word from the box.

1. A _____ person is a well-known person.

2. Something that is suddenly exciting is _____ .

3. _____ means visited many places on a trip.

4. A _____ makes books, magazines, or newspapers.

5. If you gave someone the confidence to do something, you _____ them.

Write each sentence that is true.

   A person who toured Florida visited only one city.
   A person who toured Florida visited many cities.

6. _____

   The publisher prints books about cats and dogs.
   The publisher treats sick cats and dogs in his office.

7. _____

   It is thrilling to clean your room.
   It is thrilling to go sledding in the snow.

8. _____

   Bessie's friend encouraged her to go to flight school.
   Bessie's friend encouraged her to go to cooking school.

9. _____

Unit 8   Wings

Name _____   Date _____

EXTENDING VOCABULARY

Use with textbook page 191.

Using Key Words

Read each Key Word. Then read the words that mean almost the same as the Key Word.

Key Words	Words That Mean Almost the Same
encouraged	urged inspired
famous	well-known renowned
publisher	producer of books, magazines, or newspapers
thrilling	exciting spine-tingling
toured	traveled around visited many places

Read each sentence and look at the underlined word or words. Write the Key Word that means the same as the underlined word or words.

1. Last summer, my family <u>traveled around</u> the South.

   _____

2. We visited a <u>renowned</u> theme park.

   _____

3. I was afraid to ride the roller coaster, but my brother <u>urged</u> me to try it.

   _____

4. The roller coaster ride was so <u>exciting</u> that I screamed.

   _____

5. When I got off the ride, a <u>producer of books, magazines, or newspapers</u> asked if he could use my picture in a magazine about roller coasters.

   _____

Write a sentence. Use a Key Word in your sentence.

6. _____

   _____

   _____

Name _____ Date _____

READING STRATEGY

Use with textbook page 191.

Summarize

To **summarize** means to write the main ideas in your own words. Follow these steps when you summarize what you read.

- As you read, summarize each section.
- Keep your summary simple. Be sure to use your own words.
- After you finish reading the entire text, reread your summaries. This will help you understand and remember the main ideas of the selection.

Read this paragraph from "Bessie Coleman, American Flyer." Then read the summary that appears below it.

> Bessie Coleman was born into a large family in Atlanta, Texas, on January 26, 1892. She grew up in a time of discrimination. In the South, African Americans couldn't go to school with white people. They couldn't eat at the same table or ride in the same train car. Life was very hard.

Summary

> Bessie Coleman grew up in Texas. Discrimination made her life very difficult.

Now read this paragraph. Write a short summary of what you read.

> When she was twenty-three, Bessie moved to Chicago to live with her brother. She hoped to find a better life there. Soon her mother and three younger sisters moved to Chicago, too. Bessie loved the excitement of the big city. She watched the great musician Louis Armstrong and other talented African-American performers play jazz. Chicago was an exciting place to be.

Summary

_____

_____

_____

Unit 8   Wings   175

Name _____ Date _____

VOCABULARY BUILDING

Use after the vocabulary lesson.

Nouns and Verbs

A **noun** is a word that names a person, a place, or a thing. A **verb** can show a state of being or an action.

Sometimes a word can be used as a noun or a verb.

Nouns	Verbs
a stamp	stamp
work	work
a sail	sail

Read these sentence pairs. Then write *Noun* if the underlined word is used as a noun in the sentence. Write *Verb* if the underlined word is used as a verb in the sentence.

1. Bessie Coleman had a wish that eventually came true. _____

   Many young people wish to become pilots and fly airplanes. _____

2. In an air show, pilots show the many tricks they can do. _____

   Jake and his father went to see an air show last Saturday. _____

3. Jake's dad looked at his watch. _____

   Dad and Jake were ready to watch a thrilling show. _____

4. Last week the pilot had to order missing airplane parts. _____

   The order was shipped and delivered in just three days. _____

5. Before the show, the pilot had to start the engine. _____

   If the engine has a good start, the pilot can take off. _____

6. Jake thought it might rain. _____

   A lot of rain can stop a performance. _____

176 Unit 8 Wings

Name _____ Date _____

PHONICS

Use after the phonics lesson.

One-, Two-, Three-, and Four-Syllable Words; Initial, Medial, and Final Schwa

A **syllable** is a single spoken sound that forms a word or a part of a word. Say each word aloud, and then write the number of syllables on the line.

1. schoolhouse _____
2. toured _____
3. accomplishments _____
4. reporter _____
5. twenty _____

6. family _____
7. paper _____
8. American _____
9. train _____
10. performers _____

Words that have more than one syllable may have a **schwa** sound. Listen for the schwa sound, /ə/, in these words. The schwa sound may be spelled by the letters *a, e, i, o,* or *u*.

    about   tal**e**nt   acc**i**dent   instruct**o**r   foc**us**

Listen for the schwa sound as you say the words in each row aloud, or your teacher says them. Write the word in each row that has a schwa sound in one of its syllables.

11. pencils   note   read   _____
12. place   different   math   _____
13. time   went   helmet   _____
14. find   pilot   stop   _____
15. honor   same   home   _____
16. around   with   dream   _____
17. shows   flower   flight   _____
18. finally   fly   wrote   _____

Unit 8   Wings

Name _____ Date _____

PHONICS

Use after the phonics lesson.

oo in *look* and oo in *food*

The letters *oo* can stand for the vowel sound you hear in *look*.

    g**oo**d   b**oo**k   w**oo**l

The letters *oo* can also stand for the vowel sound you hear in *food*.

    m**oo**d   z**oo**m   c**oo**l

Underline the word that is spelled with *oo* in each sentence and write the word.

1. I read a great book to my little sister. _____
2. It was about a little schoolhouse. _____
3. It only had one room. _____
4. All the children from the neighborhood went there. _____
5. The children came at seven and went home at noon. _____
6. There was a seat for every child, so no one stood. _____
7. It was good place to learn together. _____
8. Everyone was in a happy mood when the teacher read a story. _____

Write each word that you wrote above under the correct heading.

oo in *look*	oo in *food*

Unit 8   Wings

COMPREHENSION

Use with textbook page 196.

"Bessie Coleman, American Flyer"
Write a word from the box to complete each sentence in the paragraphs about Bessie Coleman.

African-American	performed
flight	cotton
France	flying
pilots	Chicago
Texas	license

Bessie Coleman was born in Atlanta, _____ **1.** _____, in 1892. As a child, she worked in the _____ **2.** _____ fields with her family. She went to a one-room school for _____ **3.** _____ children.

When she was twenty-three, Bessie moved to _____ **4.** _____ and got a job in a barber shop. Bessie listened to the war stories of men who had been _____ **5.** _____ in France. She dreamed of _____ **6.** _____ a plane, but _____ **7.** _____ schools were all-white and all-male.

Bessie's friend Robert Abbott encouraged her to go to flight school in _____ **8.** _____ . So, Bessie went to France, and got her international pilot's _____ **9.** _____ . When she came back to the United States, she _____ **10.** _____ in thrilling air shows. Bessie was killed when she fell from her plane while performing. Today, there are flying clubs named for her.

Write the first paragraph. Use cursive writing.

_____

_____

_____

_____

Unit 8   Wings

Name _____ Date _____

GRAMMAR

Use with textbook page 200.

Imperatives

An **imperative** sentence gives an instruction, a direction, or an order. The subject of an imperative sentence is almost always *you*. The subject *you* is usually not stated. Add the word *please* to make the instruction or order more polite.

> **Please** pass the potatoes.

Underline each sentence that is an imperative.

1. Eat your vegetables.
2. The dog ate my sandwich.
3. Dan played baseball with his friends.
4. Please close the door.
5. Let me in!
6. Please be quiet.
7. We are going to visit our friends.
8. Use that hose to wash the car.

Write an imperative sentence for each situation. Choose a sentence from the box.

> Watch out for the car!   Please clean your room, Julio.
> Come in now, dear.   Turn left at the corner.

9. Julio's room is messy. Julio's mom thinks he should clean it up. She should say:

_____

10. Jin Ho is playing outside. His mother wants him to come in. She should say:

_____

11. Bianca is driving the car. Roberto wants her to make a left turn at the corner. Roberto should say:

_____

12. Wan is riding his bike in the driveway. His mother wants him to be careful not to bump the car. She should say:

_____

SKILLS FOR WRITING

Use with textbook page 201.

Writing Instructions

Here are instructions for planting watermelons.

How to Plant Watermelons
1. Use a hoe to break up the garden soil.
2. Work fertilizer into the soil.
3. Rake the soil smooth.
4. Plant watermelon seeds one inch deep and six feet apart.
5. Water every morning.

Write each instruction next to the drawing that explains it. Use cursive writing.

1. _____

2. _____

3. _____

4. _____

5. _____

Unit 8   Wings

Name _____   Date _____

SPELLING

Use after the spelling lesson.

Words with Schwa

The **schwa** sound, /ə/, can be spelled with the letters *a, e, i, o,* or *u.*

Complete each word with the missing letter to spell the schwa sound.

a	e	i	o	u
__bout	childr__n	d__rection	lem__n	foc__s
wom__n	goggl__s	penc__ls	pil__t	awf__l

Use the words you wrote. Complete each word below.

1. Write the word that means more than one child.   __ __ __ __ __ __ e __

2. Write the word that means a person who flies an airplane.   __ __ __ o __

3. Write the word for things you use to write or draw with.   __ __ __ __ i __ __

4. Write the word for what pilots wear to protect their eyes.   __ __ __ __ __ e __

5. Write the word that begins with *a* and ends in *t*.   a __ __ __ __

6. Write the word that tells what you do to a camera lens.   __ __ __ u __

7. Write the word that begins with *w* and ends with *n*.   __ __ __ a __

8. Write the word that means *terrible*.   __ __ __ u __

9. Write the word for a sour-tasting fruit.   __ __ __ o __

10. Write the word that begins with *d* and ends with *n*.   __ i __ __ __ __ __ __ __

VOCABULARY

Use with textbook page 205.
"Aaron's Gift"

Key Words
broken   grabbed   leaped   soothe   wounded

▲ leaped and grabbed

▲ a wounded bird with a broken wing

▲ gently soothe

Complete each sentence with a Key Word from the box. Use the pictures to help you.

1. If someone is _____, they are hurt and need medical help.

2. Another word for *jumped* is _____.

3. If something is _____, it is damaged or not working.

4. To _____ someone means to help him or her become calm and quiet.

5. _____ means took hold of suddenly.

Write each sentence that is true.

  A wounded bird can fly very high.
  A wounded bird cannot fly.

6. _____

  You would soothe a crying baby to quiet her.
  You would soothe a sleeping dog to make it angry.

7. _____

  It is easy to walk with a broken leg.
  It is difficult to walk with a broken leg.

8. _____

Unit 8   Wings

Name _____ Date _____

READING STRATEGY

Use with textbook page 205.

Understand an Author's Purpose

Authors write fiction for many purposes, or reasons. An **author's purpose** may be to entertain or teach readers something.

- Think about the author's purpose for writing the story.
- Make a chart to write down important words and details.
- Reread the story to find another purpose the author may have had.

One purpose of the paragraph below might be to entertain. Think about this purpose as you read the paragraph. Then read the chart. Notice the words and details the author used.

    Aaron wanted to give Grandma something special for her birthday. He thought about what it could be. All at once, he knew. Pidge would be her present! Pidge could carry messages for her. Maybe Pidge could even make her feel better about something that happened a long time ago.

Author's purpose: To entertain
Words and details:
Pidge would be her present!
Pidge could carry messages for her.

One purpose the author may have is to teach the reader how to fix a bird's broken wing. Underline words and details in the paragraph that the author used to describe this task. Then use them to complete the chart.

    Aaron and Noreen began to fix the pigeon's wing. They used two ice-cream sticks and strips of cloth to hold the wing in place. Pidge did not move while the children fixed his broken wing. He seemed to know they were trying to help him.

Author's purpose: To teach how to fix a broken wing
Words and details:
_____
_____

Name _____   Date _____

GRAMMAR

Use after the grammar lesson.

Writing Dates

When **dates** are written in a text, the month is spelled out. Numerals are used for the day and the year. A comma is used to separate the day of the month and the year.

> Bessie Coleman was born on **January 26, 1892**.

When the day of the month is not written, there is no comma between the month and the year.

> Bessie returned to the United States in **September 1921**.

Underline the date in each sentence. Write the date on the line if the date is written incorrectly.

1. Christopher Columbus landed in the New World on October 12 1492. _____

2. George Washington was born on February 22, 1732. _____

3. Independence from Great Britain was declared on July 4 1776. _____

4. My grandmother came to the United States in November 1940. _____

5. The United States entered World War II in December, 1941. _____

6. On July 21, 1969, the first man set foot on the moon. _____

Write each date correctly.

7. October first 1912 _____

8. The 5th day of November in 1766 _____

9. August, 2004 _____

10. June second in the year 2003 _____

Write tomorrow's date on the line.

11. _____

Unit 8   Wings   185

COMPREHENSION

Use with textbook page 212.

"Aaron's Gift"
Write a word from the box to complete each sentence in the paragraphs about "Aaron's Gift."

| broken | carrier | badge | gift | flew |
| freedom | training | goat | birthday | strips |

In the park, Aaron found a pigeon with a _____ 1. wing. He used ice-cream sticks and _____ 2. of cloth to hold the wing in place. Aaron started _____ 3. Pidge. He wanted Pidge to be a _____ 4. pigeon.

Aaron's grandma told him about a time when she was a girl in Ukraine and had a pet _____ 5. . The Cossacks attacked her village and killed Grandma's goat. Aaron decided to give Pidge to Grandma for her _____ 6. .

Aaron wanted to join a gang. The members told him to bring his pigeon and promised him a new kind of _____ 7. . The mean boys tried to throw Pidge into a fire. Aaron fought to free Pidge, who _____ 8. away. Now, Aaron had no _____ 9. for his grandma. Soon he realized that Pidge's _____ 10. was the best gift she could have had.

Write the first paragraph of the story. Use cursive writing.

_____
_____
_____
_____
_____

Unit 8 Wings

Name _____ Date _____

GRAMMAR

Use after the grammar lesson.

Dialogue

In written **dialogue**, the speaker's words are enclosed in **quotation marks** so the reader knows these words are being spoken. The punctuation mark that goes with the spoken words is always set inside the quotation marks.

> "When is Grandma's birthday?" Noreen asked.

Underline the sentence in each pair that is dialogue.

1. "Please go to the store and get some milk," Mother said.

   I am going to the store now.

2. Aaron wanted to go to his friend's house.

   "May I please go to my friend's house?" Aaron asked his mother.

Correct each line of dialogue by rewriting it on the line. Use quotation marks to show the words being spoken.

3. That's your new name, Aaron whispered softly.

   _____

4. What is wrong with the bird? asked Noreen.

   _____

5. The bird has a broken wing, said Aaron.

   _____

6. What a sad little bird! cried Noreen.

   _____

7. Can I help you fix his wing? Noreen asked.

   _____

Unit 8   Wings

Name _____ Date _____

SPELLING PATTERNS
Use after the spelling lesson.

Double-Letter Words: *ll, tt, nn, mm, oo*
Many words have a double-letter spelling pattern.

    ba**ll**   ba**tt**alion   ru**nn**ing   su**mm**arize   st**oo**p

Underline the word in each sentence that has a double-letter spelling pattern. Write the word in cursive.

1. The people in Grandma's village got some bad news. _____
2. The czar's soldiers were coming to attack them. _____
3. Grandma's family quickly hid in the cellar. _____
4. They heard the sound of horses running. _____
5. Then they heard the soldiers slamming all their things. _____
6. When she came out, Grandma looked at her goat. _____

Write a rhyming word from the box for each word below.

better	dinner	slammed	fall	stunning	book	soothe
teller	broom	butter	good	planned	swimmer	still

7. letter _____   14. stood _____
8. cellar _____   15. call _____
9. running _____   16. tanned _____
10. jammed _____   17. flutter _____
11. look _____   18. smooth _____
12. winner _____   19. shimmer _____
13. room _____   20. thrill _____

GRAMMAR

Use with textbook page 216.

Subject-Verb Agreement: Simple Present
The **subject** and the **verb** of a sentence must agree in number. If the subject of the sentence is **singular**, then the verb should end in -s or -es. If the subject is **plural**, the verb should not end in -s or -es.

Singular: The **boy goes** to school.
Plural: **Boys go** to school.

Underline the simple-present sentence in each pair that is correct.

1. One man read a book.   One man reads a book.
2. Two girls play a game.   Two girls plays a game.
3. Grandfather sail a boat.   Grandfather sails a boat.

Choose the correct form of the verb in parentheses and write it on the line to finish the sentence.

4. Many families (live / lives) _____ in this neighborhood.
5. Boys and girls (skate / skates) _____ in the park.
6. My grandma (like / likes) _____ to feed the birds.
7. The birds (enjoy / enjoys) _____ the tiny seeds.
8. My grandpa (wish / wishes) _____ he could stay all day.
9. We (stay / stays) _____ until the sun goes down.
10. They (walk / walks) _____ to the park every afternoon.

Unit 8   Wings

Name _____ Date _____

VOCABULARY BUILDING

Use after the vocabulary lesson.

Same Words in Six Languages
Here are some examples of words in six different languages.

English	Chinese	Hmong	Cambodian	Spanish	Vietnamese
mother	moo chin	niam	mdaay	madre	me
father	foo chin	txiv	ov puk	padre	cha
hello	nee hao	nyob zoo	suesdey	hola	xin chào
good-bye	zai jin	mus zoo	leah haey	adiós	tam biêt
rice	da me	txhuv	angkaa	arroz	gao

Read each word in English. Write the same word in your native language.

1. airplane _____   3. bird _____

2. flag _____   4. goat _____

5. Read this paragraph. Then write it in your native language.

   Hue has a pet goat named Tai. When Hue walks in the park, Tai walks with her. When people see Hue and Tai, they think Tai is a dog. When they see Tai's horns, they smile.

_____
_____
_____
_____
_____

Name _____ Date _____

SKILLS FOR WRITING

Use with textbook page 217.

Writing a Review

A **review** gives the writer's opinion about a book, a story, a movie, or a show. A review includes:

- basic information about the work: the title, the author, what the work is about
- the writer's opinion: how he or she feels about the work
- reasons and examples that support the writer's opinion
- the writer's recommendation: advice about whether or not to see or read the work

Read this review of a play. Then answer the questions below.

"Aaron's Gift," a Play, reviewed by John Lopez

I saw the production of "Aaron's Gift" given by the drama club at our school. I thought it was a wonderful play to watch. Steven Lee, who played Aaron, gave an amazing performance. He made the character of Aaron come to life. I really felt frightened and sorry for Aaron as the play went on. I also felt glad for Aaron when he made his grandmother happy. The other actors played their roles very well, too.

I was especially impressed with the costumes. The clothing looked very much like the pictures I've seen from the 1940s, the time when the story took place.

If I were you, I would try to catch the next performance, which will be given next Thursday after classes.

1. What work is being reviewed? _____

2. What did the writer think about the performance given by Steven Lee?
   _____

3. What detail did the writer give to support his ideas about the costumes?
   _____
   _____
   _____

4. Do you think you would like to see this performance? Why or why not?
   _____
   _____
   _____

Unit 8   Wings   191

Name _____ Date _____

WRITING PRACTICE
Use with textbook page 218.

Write about "Wings"
Think about the different stories and articles you read in Unit 8.

What did you learn about the life of Bessie Coleman? Write three sentences about important events in Bessie's life. Here are some words you may want to use.

| encouraged   famous   publisher   thriller   toured |

_____
_____
_____
_____
_____
_____
_____
_____

During World War I, the United States army used carrier pigeons to carry important messages. Write about how the carrier pigeon Cher Ami helped the American soldiers during a battle in France.

_____
_____
_____
_____
_____
_____
_____

192   Unit 8   Wings

Reader's Companion

READER'S COMPANION

Use with textbook pages 38–41.

Summary: "Nomads"

Nomads are people who travel from place to place. Nomads usually live in open areas such as deserts or plains. Nomads include the Bedouins of the Middle East and Mongolian nomads of Asia. The Sioux lived in North America before 1850. They hunted buffalo on the plains. The Inuit once fished and hunted in the most northern part of North America. They are no longer nomads.

Visual Summary

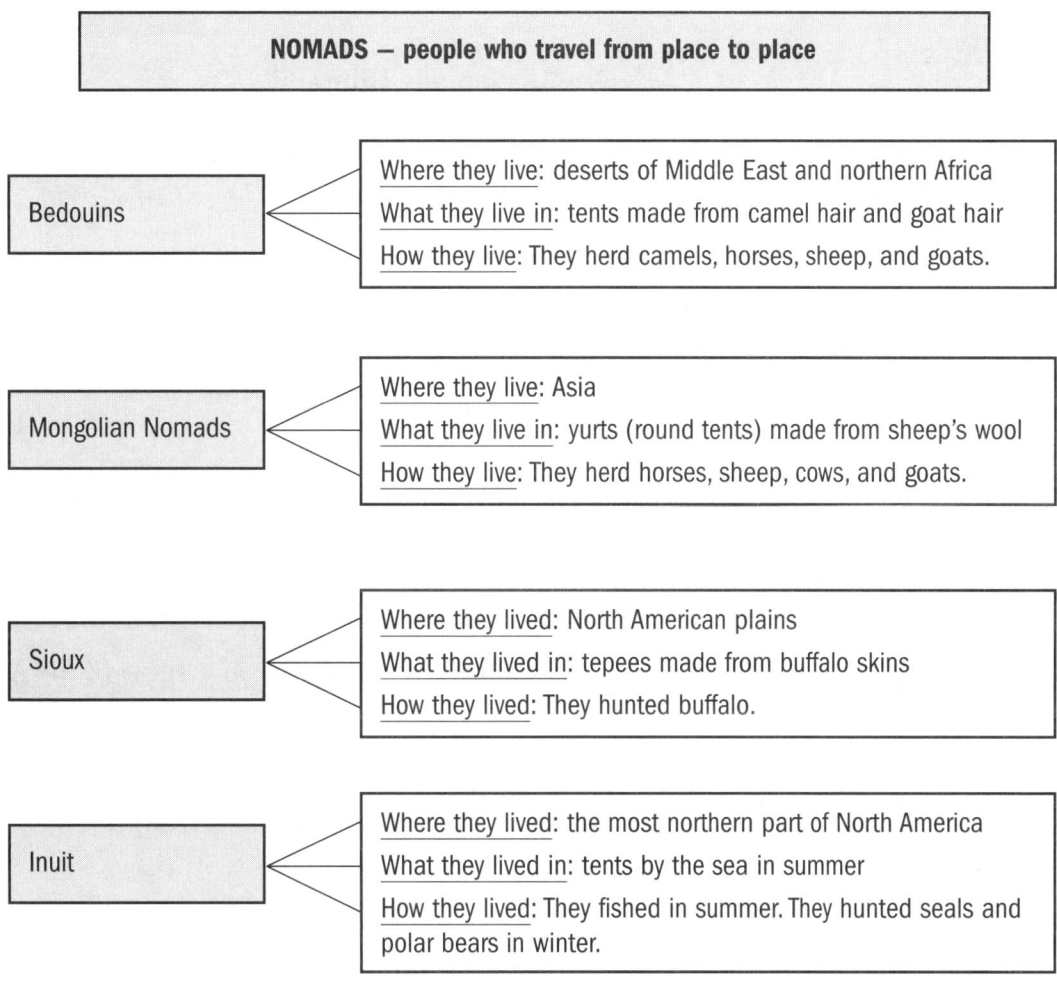

Reader's Companion   Unit 1

Name _____ Date _____

Nomads

Use What You Know
Tell three ways people find food in a place with no stores.

1. _____
   _____
2. _____
   _____
3. _____
   _____

Type of Text: Nonfiction
Nonfiction gives factual, or true, information. Circle the word that tells what most nomads are today. What large family groups do most nomads travel in?

MARK THE TEXT

_____
_____

Check Your Understanding
What are grassy plains?

_____
_____

What Are Nomads?

Nomads are people who do not live in one place. They move from place to place to find food and water. They carry their homes with them on their **journeys**. In **prehistoric** times most people were nomads. They hunted animals and looked for seeds and plants to eat.

Are All Nomads Hunters?

Some nomads today are hunters, but most are herders. They travel with herds of sheep, goats, or camels. They look for places that have grass and water for their animals. These nomads often live in tents. They travel in large family groups called tribes.

Where Do Nomads Live?

Most nomads live on open land. Some live in the desert. Others live on **grassy plains**. In the past, nomads also lived in the ice and snow of the Arctic.

_____
journeys, long trips
prehistoric, before people started writing down history
grassy plains, large areas of land where grass grows

Who Are the Bedouins?

The Bedouins (BED-oo-inz) are desert nomads. They travel across the deserts of the Middle East and northern Africa. They have herds of camels. Camels are good desert animals because they can go many days without food or water.

Some Bedouins camp near water. Then they can keep horses, sheep, and goats. The women make tents and rugs from camel hair and goat hair. Bedouin families camp in groups called clans. The clan leader is called a sheik. Many clans together make a tribe.

Who Are Mongolian Nomads?

Mongolian (mon-GO-lee-un) nomads live in Asia. They travel with herds of horses, sheep, cows, and goats. They live in round tents called yurts. Yurts are made of wool from sheep. Yurts protect the nomads from bad weather.

Mongolian nomads are famous horseback riders. Men and women ride horses and shoot arrows for fun. Young children even learn to race horses.

Reading Strategy: Preview

To preview is to look at pages before you read them. Preview this page. What new word do you think you will learn on this page?

_____

Check Your Understanding

What can Bedouins do if they camp near water? Circle the answer. Then explain the answer.

_____
_____
_____

Language Link

Sometimes you can learn a word's meaning from the words around it. Look at the word *yurts* in the third paragraph. Underline the words around it that tell what it means. What are yurts made of?

_____

Name _____ Date _____

Check Your Understanding

Read the question (heading) in dark type. Then underline the sentence in the paragraph that answers the question.

Type of Text: Nonfiction

Nonfiction gives true information about real people. Put boxes around the people that the first and second paragraphs are about. What animals did each of these people hunt?

_____
_____
_____

Check Your Understanding

Circle the sentence that tells the places where most Inuit live today. Then explain why this means they are no longer nomads.

_____
_____
_____
_____

Are There Nomads in North America?

There are very few nomads left in North America. Before 1850, there were many nomads. The Sioux (SOO), for example, hunted buffalo on the plains. They used buffalo meat for food. They made tents and blankets from buffalo skins. The tents were called tepees.

The Inuit (IN-yoo-it), who live in the most northern part of North America, were also nomads. In summer they lived in tents by the sea and fished. In winter they hunted seals and polar bears. They used small boats called kayaks. Today most Inuit live in towns or villages. They are no longer nomads.

> Photocopy a map from a book. Or print out a map from the Internet. On the map, mark the areas where the nomads you learned about live or lived.

READER'S COMPANION

Use with textbook pages 68–71.

Summary: "Earthquakes"

The layer of rock that covers the earth is called the earth's crust. Usually earthquakes happen along faults in the crust. Faults are places where huge pieces of the crust, called plates, press against one another. They press and press until one plate pushes past the other. When that happens, the ground shakes and sometimes cracks. That is an earthquake.

Visual Summary

1. Two plates of the earth's crust meet at a fault.

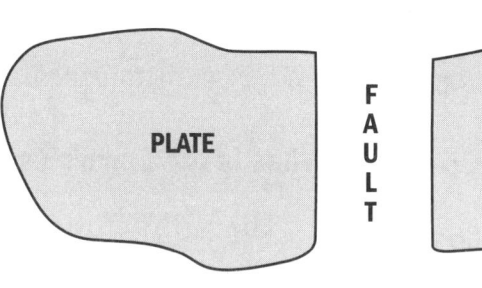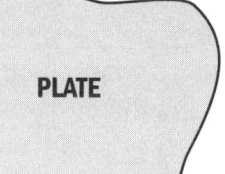

2. Pressure builds at the fault as one plate pushes against another.

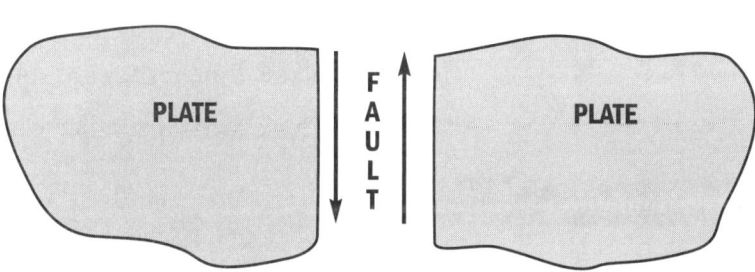

3. When one plate pushes past the other, the earth shakes—it is an earthquake.

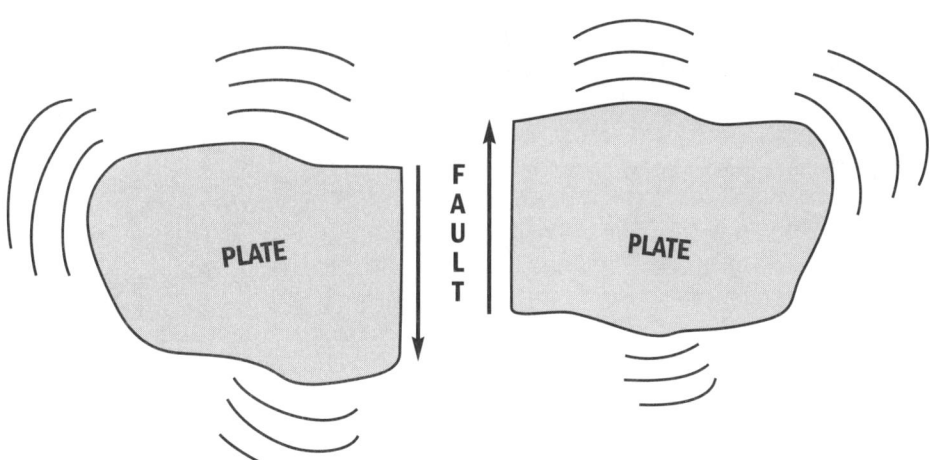

Name _____ Date _____

Earthquakes

What Is an Earthquake?

An earthquake is a sudden moving or shaking of the ground. *Quake* is another word for *shake*. Earthquakes can be mild or very powerful. Powerful earthquakes can destroy buildings and bridges. They can also cause rivers to change direction. Earthquakes under the ocean can cause huge waves, called tsunamis (soo-NAH-meez), to crash onto the land. Few earthquakes last more than thirty seconds.

What Is the Earth's Crust?

The earth's crust is a layer of rock that covers the earth. It is underneath all the land and water on the earth. The crust is made of huge pieces of rock called plates. The plates move very slowly. Where the plates touch, they can push against each other. These areas are called faults.

Use What You Know

Think about earthquakes you have seen on TV or in person. List two things that happened.

1. _____
   _____

2. _____
   _____

Reading Strategy: Look for Causes and Effects

A cause tells why something happens. An effect is what happens from a cause. Circle the event that causes rivers to change direction. Then explain what can cause a huge wave called a tsunami. **MARK THE TEXT**

_____
_____

Type of Text: Nonfiction

Nonfiction tells factual, or true, information. Underline the words that tell what the earth's crust is. Then explain what a fault is. **MARK THE TEXT**

_____
_____

200   Reader's Companion   Unit 2

Name _____   Date _____

What Happens along the Faults?

Along the faults, the rocks press together. The pressure builds up between the plates until one of the plates snaps past the other. This causes the rock along the faults to shake. The shaking is an earthquake. During an earthquake, the earth's crust can crack. These huge cracks usually happen along the faults.

Where Do Earthquakes Happen?

Most earthquakes happen along the faults, where the plates meet. One of the places where earthquakes happen is Turkey, where the city of Troy once was. Other places where earthquakes happen include Mexico, Japan, and California. As you can see, earthquakes can happen all over the world!

_____
pressure, force created by pressing

Reading Strategy: Look for Causes and Effects

Remember, a cause is why something happens. What it causes is an effect. Circle what causes one plate to snap past the other. What is the effect of one plate pushing past the other? **MARK THE TEXT**

_____
_____
_____

Check Your Understanding

The second paragraph says earthquakes can happen all over the world. Underline four places where earthquakes happen. Where was the city of Troy? **MARK THE TEXT**

_____
_____

Reading Strategy: Look for Causes and Effects

There is no city of Troy anymore. What do you think may have caused the end of Troy? Why?

_____
_____
_____
_____

Reader's Companion   Unit 2

Name _____ Date _____

Type of Text: Nonfiction

Nonfiction tells about real places and events. Put a box around the place where the San Andreas Fault is. Then underline the names of the two plates that meet at the San Andreas Fault. **MARK THE TEXT**

Check Your Understanding

What makes the San Andreas Fault different from other faults? Circle the answer. Then explain why earthquakes along this fault are more dangerous than other earthquakes. **MARK THE TEXT**

_____
_____
_____

Language Link

The Greek root *graph* means "writing." How is a *seismograph* "earthquake writing"?

_____
_____
_____

What Is the San Andreas Fault?

The San Andreas Fault in California is famous. It is where the Pacific plate slides against the North American plate. Earthquakes along this fault usually happen closer to the earth's surface than at other places. They cause more shaking. These types of earthquakes are more dangerous than ones deep under the ground.

How Do We Measure Earthquakes?

We measure earthquakes by using a special machine called a seismograph (SIZE-moh-graf). The word *seismograph* comes from the Greek word *seismos*, which means "earthquake." Earthquakes cause waves to pass through the earth's crust. Stronger earthquakes make bigger waves, and weaker earthquakes make smaller waves. A seismograph records the size of the waves and how far away the earthquake is.

> Pretend you are making a movie about an earthquake. Find music or sound effects that you think would go with an earthquake. Play the music or sound effects in class.

READER'S COMPANION

Use with textbook pages 90–92.

Summary: "Robert Clemente"

Roberto Clemente was born in Puerto Rico. He loved baseball as a boy. Later he played so well that he was asked to join the major leagues. Clemente became a star for the Pittsburgh Pirates. In 1971, when the Pirates won the World Series, he was voted Most Valuable Player. In 1972, Clemente became only the eleventh major league player to get three thousand hits. That winter, an earthquake hit Nicaragua. He was flying there to help when his plane crashed. After he died, Clemente was elected to the Baseball Hall of Fame.

Visual Summary

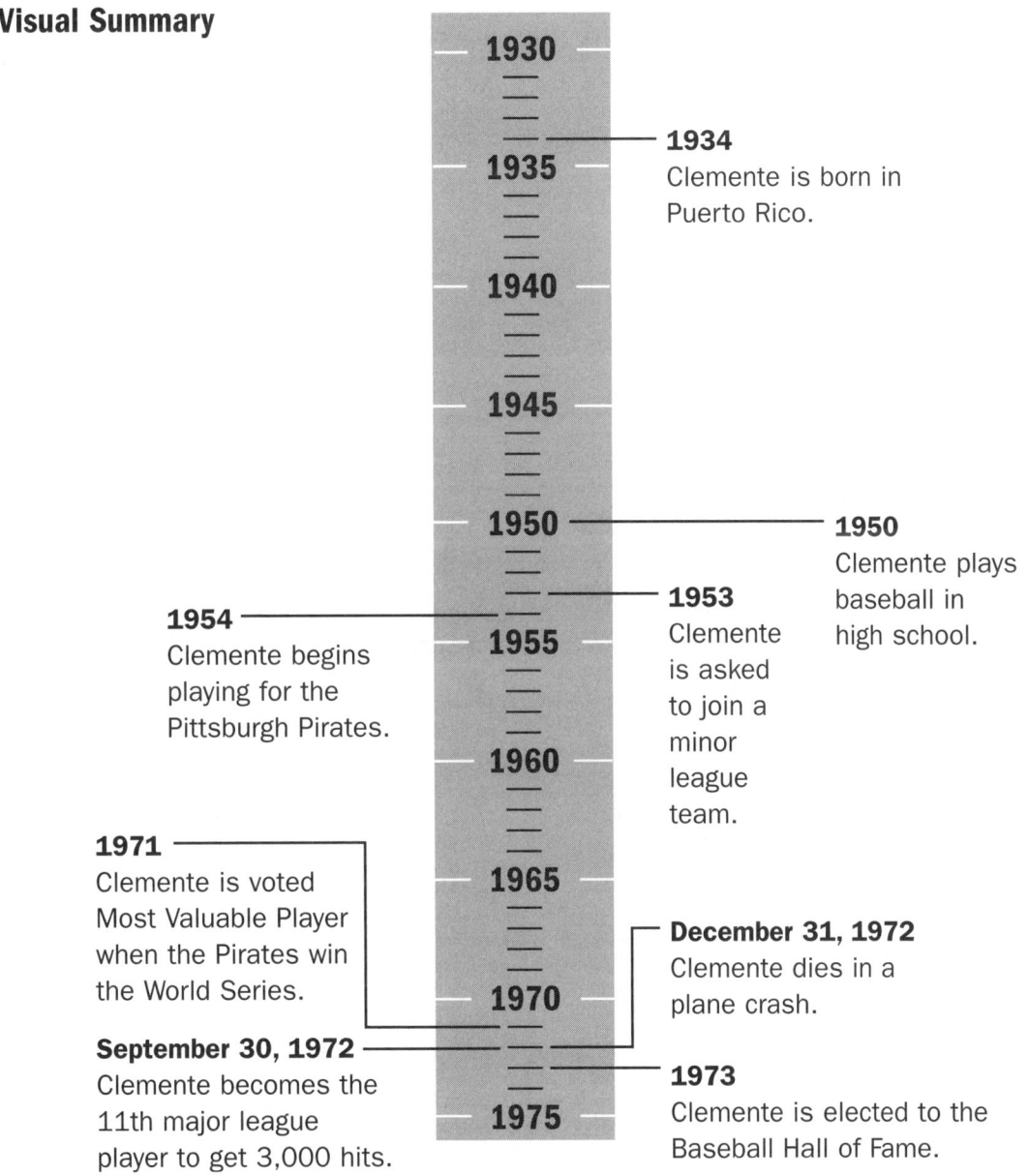

1934 Clemente is born in Puerto Rico.

1950 Clemente plays baseball in high school.

1953 Clemente is asked to join a minor league team.

1954 Clemente begins playing for the Pittsburgh Pirates.

1971 Clemente is voted Most Valuable Player when the Pirates win the World Series.

September 30, 1972 Clemente becomes the 11th major league player to get 3,000 hits.

December 31, 1972 Clemente dies in a plane crash.

1973 Clemente is elected to the Baseball Hall of Fame.

Reader's Companion   Unit 3   203

Use What You Know

Who is your favorite sports star? Write the person's name. Then write two reasons why you like him or her.

_____
_____
_____
_____

Type of Text: Biography

A biography tells the true story of a person's life. Circle the name of the person that this biography is about. What event in this person's life does the biography tell about first?

MARK THE TEXT

_____

Reading Strategy: Understand Chronological Order

This biography is told in chronological order, or time order. Underline the words that tell what happened to Robert Clemente in 1953. What happened the next year?

MARK THE TEXT

_____
_____
_____

Roberto Clemente

Roberto Clemente was born in Carolina, Puerto Rico, in 1934. His father worked on a sugar cane **plantation**, and his mother worked in a grocery store. As a boy, Roberto loved baseball. His family didn't have much money, so Roberto had to make his own baseballs. He took old golf balls and wrapped string and tape around them to make them the right size.

Roberto played baseball in high school. After high school, he played for a team in Puerto Rico. In 1953, the Brooklyn Dodgers asked Roberto to join one of their **minor league** teams in Montreal, Canada. The next year, the Pittsburgh Pirates chose him to play for them in the **major leagues**. Roberto moved to Pittsburgh, Pennsylvania, and played **right field** for the Pirates for the next eighteen years. He became one of the best players in the major leagues.

---

plantation, large farm
minor league, less important group of teams of baseball players
major leagues, most important groups of teams of baseball players
right field, position in a baseball field

His fans called him "The Great One." Roberto didn't speak English well, so reporters and sports writers sometimes made fun of him. Roberto didn't listen to them. He played great baseball and helped other Spanish-speaking players.

In 1971, the Pirates played against the Baltimore Orioles in the World Series, the games that decide the best baseball team in North America. Roberto was amazing! In seven games, he had 12 hits, including 2 home runs, 2 doubles, and 1 triple. The Pirates won the Series, and Roberto was voted Most Valuable Player of the Series.

Another of Roberto's great achievements happened on September 30, 1972. He got his three-thousandth hit as a major league player. At that time, he was only the eleventh player ever to get that many hits. But the hit was to be his last.

On December 23, 1972, three earthquakes hit the city of Managua, Nicaragua. More than 10,000 people died, and more than 250,000 people lost their homes. Most of the buildings in the city were destroyed. The city had no water, electricity, or gas. Rescue workers there needed help.

---

made fun of, laughed at, said unkind things about
home runs, hits that let the batter run around all the bases and score a run
doubles, hits that get the batter to second base
triple, hit that gets the batter to third base

Check Your Understanding

Underline the name that fans had for Roberto Clemente. What did he do to get that name?

_____
_____
_____

Language Link

Cardinal numbers show amounts. *One*, *two*, and *three* are cardinal numbers. Ordinal numbers show order. *First*, *second*, and *third* are ordinal numbers. After *first*, *second*, and *third*, the ordinal numbers end in *th*. For example, you say "This is the *fourth* game of the World Series." Circle two ordinal numbers on this page.

Reading Strategy: Understand Chronological Order

Put boxes around three dates on this page that help show chronological order. How many years after winning the World Series did Roberto Clemente hit his three-thousandth hit?

_____

Reader's Companion Unit 3

Name _____ Date _____

Type of Text: Biography

A biography tells about events in a person's life. Underline the event that the first paragraph tells about. What effect did this event have on Clemente's life?

MARK THE TEXT

_____
_____
_____

Check Your Understanding

What did Roberto Clemente want to do in Nicaragua? What kind of person was Clemente?

_____
_____
_____
_____

Check Your Understanding

What did Roberto Clemente's wife and sons do? Circle your answer. Then explain how their action honored Roberto Clemente.

MARK THE TEXT

_____
_____
_____
_____

Roberto had once said, "Anytime you have an opportunity to make things better and you don't, you are wasting your time on this earth." Roberto now had a chance to help the people of Nicaragua. On New Year's Eve, he and four friends loaded a plane with medicine and other supplies and took off from Puerto Rico to Nicaragua. But they never got there. The plane crashed into the ocean, and Roberto and his friends died.

After he died, people honored Roberto in many ways. Sports writers **elected** him to the **Baseball Hall of Fame** in 1973. He was the first player from Latin America ever to receive this honor. People all over the world named schools and hospitals after him. And his wife and sons collected money to build a sports center for children in Puerto Rico. It was something Roberto had always planned to do.

---

elected, chose
Baseball Hall of Fame, museum in New York State that honors people important to baseball

---

Draw a baseball field. If you need help, look in a book about baseball or on the Internet. Label the following: first base, second base, third base, home plate, the pitcher's mound, right field, center field, and left field.

---

206 Reader's Companion Unit 3

READER'S COMPANION

Use with textbook pages 104–106.

Summary: "The Clever Daughter-in-Law"

A rich old man wants his three sons to marry. The first two sons marry sisters from the next town. The young wives miss their mother and visit her every month. The father-in-law does not like them going away so often. He asks them to bring back two gifts: wind wrapped in paper and fire wrapped in paper. The sisters do not know what to do. But a clever farm girl helps them by solving the riddle. When the young wives explain who solved the riddle, their father-in-law invites the clever girl to meet his third son. The third son marries the clever farm girl.

Visual Summary

A rich old man tells his three sons to marry. → Two sons marry sisters from the next town. Every month the sisters visit their mother. → The father-in-law does not like the visits. He tells the sisters they can go. But he asks them to bring back two gifts: wind wrapped in paper and fire wrapped in paper.

↓

The sisters cry because they do not know how to get such gifts. A clever farm girl helps them.

↓

The father-in-law invites the clever farm girl to meet his third son. The son and the clever farm girl marry. ← The father-in-law thinks that the young wives were very clever to solve his riddle. They tell him that it was the farm girl who solved the riddle. ← The clever farm girl gives the sisters a paper fan and a paper lantern to bring back to their father-in-law.

Name _____ Date _____

Use What You Know

What do you think makes a good husband or wife? List three things you think are important.

1. _____
2. _____
3. _____

Type of Text: Folktale

"The Clever Daughter-in-Law" is a folktale—a story told by folk, or people. People around the world tell folktales. What country is this folktale from? Circle the answer. **MARK THE TEXT**

Reading Strategy: Predict

To predict is to guess what will happen in a story. When you predict, you look for clues and think about what will happen next. Do you think the old man will ask for something hard or easy for the sisters to get? Explain why. Underline a sentence in the third paragraph that gave you a clue. **MARK THE TEXT**

_____
_____
_____
_____

The Clever Daughter-in-Law

Adapted from *Celebrate the World: Twenty Tellable Folktales for Multicultural Festivals*, by Margaret Read MacDonald

Long, long ago in China, there was a rich old man. He lived in a big house. He had three sons. One day he said to his sons, "It is time for you to marry. I am getting old. I need a big family around me to help me in my old age."

Two of the sons found lovely wives. The two wives were sisters from a family in the next town. Soon the sisters came to live in the big house with their new husbands and their father-in-law. The old man was very happy. But he still needed to find a wife for his third son.

The two sisters liked the big new house, but they missed their mother terribly. Every month they wanted to visit her. "Kind Father-in-law," they said, "may we go home again for a few days?" The old man agreed, but he did not like them to go away so often.

One day the old man had an idea. The two sisters came as usual and said, "Kind Father-in-law, may we go to visit our mother for a few days?"

"Of course," said the old man. "But please bring me two gifts when you return."

"Certainly," said the young wives. They wanted to please their father-in-law. "What gifts may we bring you?" they asked.

208 Reader's Companion Unit 4

Name _____ Date _____

To the first wife the old man said, "You must bring me the wind wrapped in paper." And to the second wife he said, "You must bring me fire wrapped in paper." The two sisters were shocked. They left quickly. Then they walked along the road **silently** for some time.

"How can I find wind wrapped in paper?" the first sister asked.

"How can I find fire wrapped in paper?" asked the second sister. Neither sister had an answer. They sat down under a tree and began to cry loudly.

Soon a young farm girl saw them. She was walking with her **water buffalo**. "Why are you crying?" she asked. The sisters told her of the gifts they needed for their father-in-law. "Is that all?" the girl asked. "I can help you. Go to visit your mother and enjoy yourselves. I will have the gifts ready for you when you return."

The two sisters returned the next day. The farm girl was waiting. "Here is the wind wrapped in paper," she said. In her hand was a paper fan. It made a gentle **breeze** when she waved it. Then she said, "And here is fire wrapped in paper." This time she held up a paper lantern with a bright candle inside.

---
silently, very quietly
water buffalo, large buffalo of Asia, often used as a farm animal
breeze, mild wind

Type of Text: Folktale

This folktale has a riddle, or puzzle, in it. Underline the riddle that the father-in-law gives his two daughters-in-law. Why are the sisters shocked, or upset?

MARK THE TEXT

_____
_____
_____

Language Link

Many adverbs describe words that show action. The adverbs tell how that action happens. Often the adverbs end in -*ly*. Circle three adverbs in the first three paragraphs on this page. From each, draw an arrow to the word that it describes.

MARK THE TEXT

Check Your Understanding

Put a box around each of the two gifts that solve the riddle. How is the first gift like wind wrapped in paper?

MARK THE TEXT

_____
_____
_____

Reader's Companion   Unit 4

Name _____ Date _____

Reading Strategy: Predict

What do you predict will happen to the farm girl in the end? Why? Explain how the story's title gives you a clue.

_____
_____
_____

Check Your Understanding

What does the old man do when he finds out about the clever farm girl? Circle your answer. Then explain why he feels lucky in the end.

MARK THE TEXT

_____
_____
_____
_____

Type of Text: Folktale

In folktales, poor or common people often use their brains to do well in the end. Explain how that happens in this folktale. Why do you think most people like endings like the one in this story?

_____
_____
_____
_____
_____

"What a clever girl you are!" said the sisters. "Thank you so much!" They took the gifts and walked quickly back to the big house.

"Did you bring me the gifts?" asked the old man.

"Yes, good Father-in-law," said the two wives.

"Here is the wind wrapped in paper," said the first wife, and she showed him the fan.

"And here is fire wrapped in paper," said the second wife, and she showed him the lantern.

"How clever you are!" said the old man. "How did you think of these things?"

"Oh, we are not the clever ones," they said. "The young girl with the water buffalo was the clever one."

The old man invited the clever girl to meet his third son. They liked each other right away. Soon they married.

"How lucky I am," said the old father. "Now I have a happy house and a clever new daughter-in-law."

Paper fans and lanterns often have drawings on them. Make your own paper fan or lantern, or draw a picture of one. On your fan or lantern, draw or paint a scene from the story.

READER'S COMPANION

Use with textbook pages 134–136.

Summary: "The Great Minu"

A young man named Akwasi travels from his village in Ghana to Accra, the country's capital. He does not know that the people there speak a different language. He sees many fine things and asks who owns them. Each time he is told, "Minu," which means, "I don't understand." But he thinks the people are answering his questions and that Minu is a person—in fact, a very rich man. Then Akwasi passes a funeral and asks a woman who has died. She says, "Minu." Akwasi decides that it is not so bad to be just plain Akwasi and not the great Mr. Minu.

Visual Summary

What Akwasi Asks	What People Say	What It Means	What Akwasi Thinks
Who owns all these cows?	Minu.	I don't understand.	Mr. Minu owns all the cows. He must be a very rich man.
Who owns all these beautiful shops?	Minu.	I don't understand.	Mr. Minu owns the shops. He must be very, very rich.
Who owns these houses?	Minu.	I don't understand.	Mr. Minu owns the houses. Of course, the great Mr. Minu!
Who owns these ships?	Minu.	I don't understand.	Mr. Minu owns the ships. He must be the richest man in the world.
Who is the person who died?	Minu.	I don't understand.	Mr. Minu has died, just like any other person. It is not so bad to be plain Akwasi, and not the great Minu.

Name _____ Date _____

Use What You Know

Think of a situation in which one person didn't understand what another said. Tell what happened.

_____
_____
_____
_____

Type of Text: Folktale

People all over the world tell folktales. Circle the country this folktale comes from. Where does Akwasi live? Where does Akwasi go?

_____
_____
_____

Reading Strategy: Understand Irony

Sometimes you know something that a character in the story doesn't know. This is called irony. Underline what *Minu* means in the language of Accra. What does Akwasi think *Minu* means?

_____
_____
_____

The Great Minu

Adapted from *Folktales and Fairy Tales of Africa*, selected and retold by Lila Green

A long time ago, there was a young man named Akwasi (ah-KWAH-zee). Akwasi lived in a small village in Ghana. One day, Akwasi decided to travel to Accra, the capital city. It was a long way from his village. He had never been to Accra before. He did not know that the people of Accra spoke a different language.

Akwasi walked for many days. Finally, he arrived at the city of Accra. Just outside the city were hundreds of cows.

"Tell me, who owns all these cows?" he asked a young boy who was standing near the cows.

"Minu," the boy said, which in the language of Accra means, "I don't understand."

"Minu?" Akwasi said. "Minu must be a very rich man!"

Then Akwasi entered the city. He saw many big shops. The shops were full of beautiful things—rugs, gold jewelry, bells, lamps, and mirrors. In his small village, there were no shops like these.

Akwasi asked a woman, "Tell me, who owns all these beautiful shops?"

But the woman did not understand. "Minu," she said.

"Mr. Minu?" Akwasi said. "He owns all these shops, too? He really must be very, very rich!"

212   Reader's Companion   Unit 5

Next, Akwasi walked by some very large and fine houses.

"These houses are magnificent," he said. "They are not like the small huts in my village!"

Akwasi saw a young girl sweeping the steps of a big house.

"Tell me, who owns these houses?" he asked.

But the young girl did not understand. "Minu," she said.

"Minu," Akwasi repeated. "Of course, the great Mr. Minu!"

Then Akwasi arrived at the port. There were many ships. Akwasi could see that there were many boxes and bags of grain on the ships.

"Tell me, who owns all these ships?" Akwasi asked a sailor.

But the sailor did not understand. "Minu," he said.

"Is that so?" Akwasi said. "Mr. Minu owns these ships, too? Mr. Minu must be the richest man in the whole world!"

After Akwasi had walked around Accra for a long, long time, he decided to go home. He wanted to be back in his own village. He began walking toward the edge of the city. Suddenly, he saw a long line of people. They were walking behind a coffin. Many of the people were crying.

---
magnificent, grand, beautiful
huts, small houses with only one or two rooms

Check Your Understanding
Circle the word that Akwasi uses to describe the houses. How do you think Akwasi feels about Mr. Minu and all he owns?

Reading Strategy: Understand Irony
Irony happens when the reader knows something that a character in the story doesn't know. Irony can make a story funny. Put a box around the word that Akwasi still doesn't understand. Then tell how irony makes this story funny.

Language Link
Sometimes you can figure out the meaning of a word by looking at the words around it. Look at the words near the word *coffin*. Underline any words that give clues to its meaning. What do you think the word *coffin* means?

Reading Strategy: Understand Irony

Remember, irony happens when you know something that a character doesn't know. Underline the mistakes Akwasi makes in the next-to-last paragraph. Even though he makes these mistakes, what important lesson does Akwasi learn?

_____
_____
_____

Type of Text: Folktale

Most folktales are about poor, common people. Sometimes those people are clever, but sometimes they are not. Which kind of person is Akwasi? Explain your answer.

_____
_____
_____

"A funeral," Akwasi said to himself. "An important person must have died."

Akwasi stopped a woman who was in the long line of people. "Tell me," he said. "Who is the person who died?" But the woman did not understand.

"Minu," she said sadly.

"Oh, no!" Akwasi said. "The great Mr. Minu is dead! Can it be true? How sad! He owned hundreds of cows. He owned many beautiful shops. He owned magnificent houses. He owned many large ships. And now look at him! He is in a coffin. He has left all those fine things behind. He has died, just like any other person."

At that moment, Akwasi felt that it was not so bad to be just plain Akwasi, and not the great Mr. Minu. The more he thought about it, the more Akwasi understood that he had much to be thankful for. Akwasi felt that it was very good to be alive, even if he didn't own a lot of things. And so Akwasi walked back to his village, a happy man.

Draw a map of the city of Accra. Show the places that Akwasi visits. Include simple pictures of the things he sees on his trip.

READER'S COMPANION

Use with textbook pages 148–150 and 153.

Summary: "The Blind Men and the Elephant"

Six blind men in India meet an old man with an elephant. Not knowing about elephants, the men each touch the animal to learn about it. They each touch a different part of the elephant and so get a different idea of what it is like. When the men argue, the old man explains that an elephant is more than the parts each man has touched: It is all those things put together—it is something huge and strange!

Visual Summary

What is an elephant like?

1st Blind Man: An elephant is like a spear.	2nd Blind Man: An elephant is like a snake.	3rd Blind Man: An elephant is like a tree.
4th Blind Man: An elephant is like a wall.	5th Blind Man: An elephant is like a fan.	6th Blind Man: An elephant is like a rope.

An elephant is all those things put together.

Summary: "Rain Poem"

The poem compares rain to a mouse.

Visual Summary

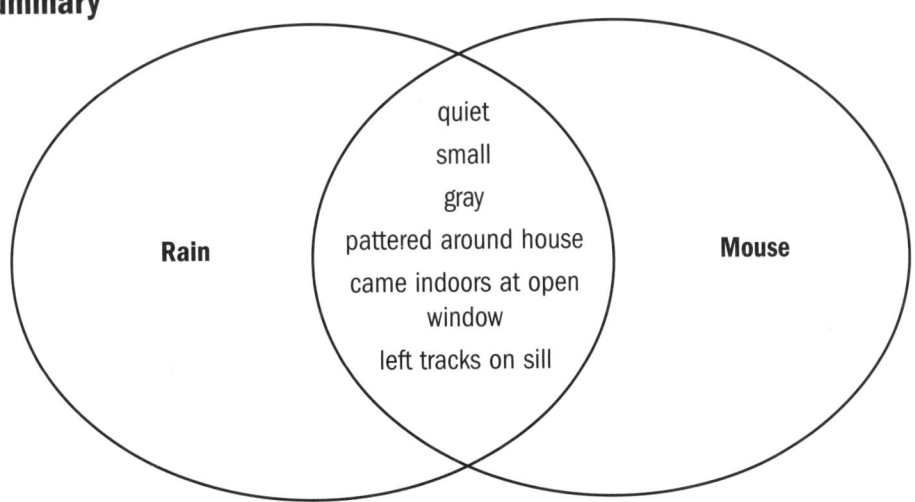

Rain / Mouse
- quiet
- small
- gray
- pattered around house
- came indoors at open window
- left tracks on sill

Reader's Companion   Unit 6

Name _____ Date _____

Use What You Know

How would you describe an animal to someone who has never seen it? Write two or three sentences describing any animal. See if your classmates can guess what it is.

_____
_____
_____
_____
_____

Type of Text: Fable

"The Blind Men and the Elephant" is a fable. A fable is a story that teaches a lesson about life. Fables come from all over the world. Circle the word that tells where this fable is from.

MARK THE TEXT

Check Your Understanding

What does the first blind man think an elephant is like? What does the second blind man think an elephant is like? Why?

_____
_____
_____
_____
_____
_____

The Blind Men and the Elephant

Once upon a time, six blind men were walking down a road in India. They met an old man leading an elephant. They stopped to speak to the old man. One of the blind men said, "Sir, what kind of animal do you have? It is making a strange noise."

The old man said, "It is an elephant."

"An elephant?" said one of the blind men. "I don't know what an elephant is."

"May we touch it?" asked the second blind man. "We want to know what an elephant is like."

"Of course," said the old man. "This elephant is gentle. It will not hurt you."

One by one, the blind men began to touch the elephant. The first blind man touched one of the elephant's tusks. It was long and smooth. The tip was pointed and sharp. He said, "An elephant is like a spear."

Then the second blind man touched the elephant's trunk. It was long and very strong. It moved up and down and from side to side. He cried, "Brothers, an elephant is not like a spear. It is like a snake!"

---

strange, not usual

216   Reader's Companion   Unit 6

Name _____ Date _____

Next, the third blind man touched one of the elephant's legs. It felt thick and rough. It was very tall. "No, you are wrong, my brothers. An elephant is not like a spear. It is not like a snake, either. It is like a large tree."

After that, the fourth blind man touched the elephant's side. Then he said, "Are you crazy? An elephant is not like a spear. And it is not like a snake. It is not like a tree, either. It is hard and wide and flat. I cannot find the end of it. An elephant is like a great wall."

At that moment, the elephant lowered its head. The fifth blind man reached out and touched one of the elephant's ears. It felt big and soft and flat. It flapped and made a breeze. He said, "No, my brothers. An elephant is not like a spear or a snake or a tree or a wall. It is like a huge fan."

---

breeze, gentle wind

Check Your Understanding

Circle the part of the elephant that the third blind man touches. When he says the elephant is like a tree, what part of a tree does he mean? Explain your answer.

MARK THE TEXT

_____
_____
_____

Check Your Understanding

Why does the fourth blind man think the others are crazy?

_____
_____
_____

Language Link

Adjectives are words that describe people, animals, places, things, and ideas. Underline three adjectives that describe the elephant's ear. Why does the sixth blind man say the elephant is like a fan?

MARK THE TEXT

_____
_____
_____

Reader's Companion   Unit 6

Name _____ Date _____

Check Your Understanding

The old man says the six blind men are all right. He also says that they are all wrong. Explain how they can be both right and wrong.

_____
_____
_____

Reading Strategy: Make Inferences

Sometimes writers do not tell you what a story means. They want you to make inferences about, or guess, the story's meaning. They help you do this by giving you clues. Each blind man thinks he knows what an elephant is like. But each man has only one clue and does not see the big picture. You can put the clues together and see the big picture. What would you say an elephant is like?

_____
_____
_____

Type of Text: Fable

A fable is a story that teaches a moral, or a lesson about life. What lesson do you think this fable teaches? Explain.

_____
_____
_____
_____

Finally, the sixth blind man touched the elephant's tail. It was long and thin. It had hair on the end. He said, "You are all wrong. An elephant is not like a spear or a snake or a tree or a wall, or even a fan. An elephant is like a rope."

Now, the blind men started to argue. Each one thought that his idea about an elephant was correct.

"Wait," said the old man with the elephant. "You are all right. But you are also all wrong."

The six men were confused. "How can we be right—and wrong?" they asked.

The old man replied, "Each of you touched only a part of the elephant. An elephant is more than a spear. It is more than a snake. It is more than a tree. It is more than a wall. It is more than a fan. It is more than a rope. Imagine an animal that is all of those things put together. Can you imagine something huge and strange? That is an elephant."

_____
imagine, see in your mind, picture

> Draw a picture of an elephant. Label the parts that the six blind men touch. Each label should say what the part is and what the blind man thinks it is like.

218   Reader's Companion   Unit 6

Name _____ Date _____

Rain Poem

The rain was like a little mouse,
quiet, small and gray.
It pattered all around the house
and then it went away.

It did not come, I understand,
indoors at all, until
it found an open window and
left tracks across the sill.

—Elizabeth Coatsworth

_____

sill, bottom of a window

Use What You Know

How would you describe rain to someone who did not know what it was? Write a sentence or two describing it.

_____
_____
_____
_____

Type of Text: Poem

The last words in a poem's lines sometimes rhyme, or have the same end sounds. For example, *rain* and *cane* rhyme. Circle the rhyming words at the ends of lines in "Rain Poem." Draw lines connecting the words that rhyme. **MARK THE TEXT**

Check Your Understanding

A simile shows how two things are alike, or similar. It uses the word *like* to compare the two things. Underline the two things that the simile in this poem compares. Then list three ways in which the two things are similar. **MARK THE TEXT**

1. _____
_____

2. _____
_____

3. _____
_____

Reader's Companion   Unit 6

READER'S COMPANION

Use with textbook pages 178–180.

Summary: "Apollo and Daphne"

Cupid, the god of love, shot arrows that could make people fall in love. Cupid's uncle Apollo said Cupid wasn't big or strong enough to be a hunter. Cupid got angry and shot an arrow at Apollo. The arrow made Apollo fall in love with Daphne, the daughter of the river god Peneus. Daphne was afraid of Apollo. She did not love him. As she ran from him, she asked for her father's help. Peneus turned her into a laurel tree. Apollo was sad that Daphne would never be his wife. However, the tree became special to him. He wore a crown of laurel leaves in his hair and gave crowns of laurel leaves to musicians, poets, and athletes.

Visual Summary

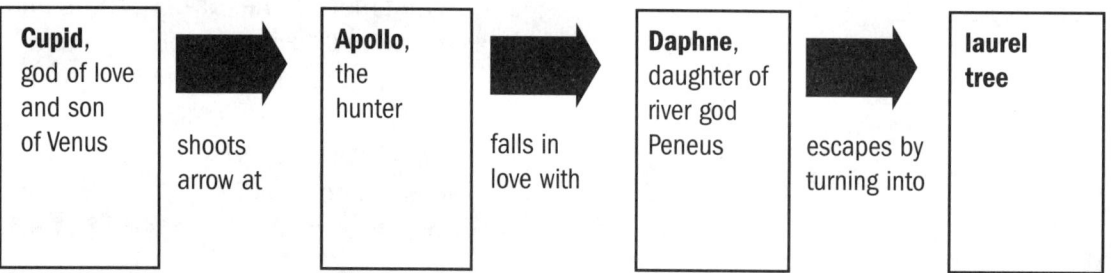

Apollo and Daphne

One day, Cupid, the young god of love, was playing with his little bow and arrows. The arrows were a gift from his mother, Venus. She was the goddess of love and beauty. Cupid's arrows were small, but they were powerful. They could make people fall in love.

Cupid wanted to be a hunter like Apollo, his uncle. However, Apollo didn't think Cupid was big and strong enough. One day, Apollo saw Cupid playing with his bow and arrows. "Put away your little arrows, Cupid," he said. "You can't be a hunter. You need to be bigger and stronger."

Apollo's words made Cupid angry. "You and your arrows are bigger," Cupid said, "but my arrows are more powerful." Cupid shot one of his arrows at Apollo and hit him. Cupid's arrow made Apollo fall in love with Daphne, the daughter of the river god, Peneus (puh-NEE-us).

Use What You Know

What do you think makes people fall in love? Write one or two sentences giving your ideas.

Type of Text: Myth

Myths are old stories that explain things in nature. Myths often include gods and goddesses. "Apollo and Daphne" is a Roman myth. Circle the word that tells what Cupid is the god of. Who is Cupid's mother?

MARK THE TEXT

Check Your Understanding

Underline what happens when Cupid's arrow hits his uncle Apollo. Why does Cupid shoot the arrow at him?

MARK THE TEXT

Reading Strategy: Visualize

To visualize, look for words that help you picture the story in your mind. Circle two or more words that help you picture what Daphne looks like.

Check Your Understanding

Underline the reason that Apollo follows Daphne. What are Daphne's reasons for running away from Apollo?

_____

_____

_____

Language Link

The comparative form of an adjective compares two people, places, or things. It often ends in -er. Put a box around a comparative form in the fourth paragraph. What two people, places, or things does it compare?

_____

Daphne was very beautiful. She had long hair and fair skin. Daphne was also very shy. She did not like talking to people, so she lived alone in the forest.

As soon as Apollo saw Daphne in the forest, he fell in love with her. He wanted to talk to her, so he followed her. Daphne was afraid and ran away from Apollo. She did not love him.

Apollo ran after her. "Daphne! Please, wait!" Apollo cried. "I love you. I am not your enemy." But Daphne did not stop. She ran farther into the forest.

They ran and ran. Daphne was fast, but Apollo was faster. Soon Daphne was tired, and Apollo came closer. Daphne called to her father, Peneus. "Father! I'm tired! You must help me!" The river god heard his daughter's voice.

"Don't worry, Daphne," he cried. "I am here. I will help you!"

Suddenly, Daphne began to change. Her feet became roots, and they grew into the earth. Her arms became branches, and her hair became leaves. Daphne's body became covered in bark. She was now a beautiful laurel tree.

Apollo was amazed. He touched her branches and leaves. "You cannot be my wife," Apollo said sadly, "but you will always be my special tree. I will wear your leaves as my crown forever."

From that day, Apollo gave laurel crowns to all the great musicians, poets, and athletes in honor of Daphne, his one great love.

Even in our time, we still give laurel crowns to honor great athletes.

Visualize the beautiful laurel tree that Daphne becomes. Or visualize another character or scene in the myth. Then draw or paint a picture of what you see in your mind.

Reading Strategy: Visualize

Remember, when you visualize, you look for words that help you picture the story in your mind. Underline the sentences that help you picture what happens to Daphne. What does Daphne become?

___

Check Your Understanding

Put boxes around two words that show Apollo's feelings about what happened to Daphne. Why will he wear laurel leaves as his crown forever?

___

Type of Text: Myth

Long ago people told myths to explain how things in nature came about or why human beings do certain things. Circle something we do that the myth helps explain. What thing in nature does the myth also explain?

___

READER'S COMPANION

Use with textbook pages 206–211.

Summary: "Aaron's Gift"

Aaron finds a hurt pigeon in a New York City park. He fixes the bird's broken wing, and his parents let him keep the bird. Aaron plans to give "Pidge" to Grandma for her birthday. When Grandma was a girl back in Ukraine, soldiers called Cossacks attacked her village and killed her pet goat. When the story was written, Ukraine was called "the Ukraine." Aaron hopes that Pidge will make Grandma feel better about her long-lost pet.

Meanwhile, Carl, the leader of a gang of older boys, tells Aaron that he can join the gang only if he brings Pidge to their clubhouse. When Aaron does this, the gang members try to hurt Pidge. Aaron fights with them, and Pidge flies away during the struggle. Aaron goes home and tells Grandma what happened. She thanks him for his gift. At first Aaron doesn't understand what she means, since Pidge flew away. Later Aaron realizes that, for Grandma, freeing Pidge was the best gift he could give her. It was as if he had saved her pet goat from the Cossacks.

Visual Summary

AARON'S GOALS			
Goal	Completed?	How It Was Completed	Why It Was Not Completed
to help a pigeon with a broken wing	Yes	Aaron uses ice-cream sticks and strips of cloth to fix the wing.	
to join a gang of older boys	No		The boys try to harm the pigeon.
to give the pigeon to his grandmother, whose goat was killed by Cossacks when she was young	No		The pigeon flies away.
to give his grandmother a gift	Yes	Freeing the pigeon was the best gift Aaron could give his grandmother.	

Name _____ Date _____

Aaron's Gift
Adapted from the story by Myron Levoy

Aaron went to Tompkins Square Park to roller-skate because the streets around his house were too crowded with children and dogs and traffic. He skated back and forth, pretending he was in a race. Then he noticed a pigeon on the grass.

The pigeon looked hurt. It tried to fly, but its left wing wouldn't flap. Aaron thought the wing looked broken. He took a cookie from his pocket and tossed some crumbs on the ground. "Here pidge, here pidge," he said.

The pigeon strutted over to eat the crumbs. Aaron pulled off his shirt. Moving slowly, he covered the wounded pigeon with his shirt and captured it. "Good pidge," he said softly. "That's your new name. Pidge."

The pigeon struggled. Aaron stroked the bird and tried to soothe it. "I'm going to take you home, Pidge," he said. "I'm going to fix you up. Easy, Pidge."

---

struggled, moved wildly

Use What You Know
Why do people have pets? What good things do pets bring to people's lives? Write two or three sentences answering these questions.

_____
_____
_____
_____
_____
_____

Type of Text: Short Story
"Aaron's Gift" is a short story. It takes place in New York City. Circle what Aaron finds in the park. Tell what is unusual about it. **MARK THE TEXT**

Check Your Understanding
Why does Aaron want to take the pigeon home? Underline the sentence that tells his reason. **MARK THE TEXT**

Reader's Companion   Unit 8

Name _____ Date _____

Language Link

Some words can have more than one meaning. The word *stoop* can mean "bend forward." It can also mean "a flat place at the top of steps leading to a building." Which do you think *stoop* means here? Explain why.

_____
_____
_____
_____

Check Your Understanding

Where did Aaron's grandmother live as a child?

_____

Language Link

Sometimes you can find out the meaning of a word by looking at the words around it. What do you think *temporarily* means? Look at the last paragraph. Underline the words that tell the meaning of *temporarily*.

MARK THE TEXT

Aaron skated out of the park and headed for home. He held the pigeon in his hands. When he reached his house, he saw his friend Noreen on the stoop. "Is he sick?" asked Noreen.

"Broken wing," Aaron responded. "I'm going to fix it. Want to help?"

"Yes, I'll help," said Noreen.

Aaron and Noreen began to fix the pigeon's wing. They used two ice-cream sticks and strips of cloth to hold the wing in place. Pidge did not move while the children fixed his broken wing. He seemed to know they were trying to help him.

Aaron wasn't sure what his mother would say about his new pet. But he knew his grandmother would be happy for him. She liked to feed crumbs to the birds on the back fire escape. Sometimes Aaron heard her talking to the birds about her childhood in the Ukraine. Aaron knew she would love Pidge.

To his surprise, Aaron's mother told him he could keep Pidge temporarily. That meant he could keep Pidge for a while. But when Aaron's father came home, he stared at the pigeon with the bandaged wing. "Who did this?" he asked.

Name _____ Date _____

"Me," said Aaron. "And Noreen."

"You're a genius!" his father said. "You're only a kid and you fixed a bird's wing. Just like a real doctor." Aaron could tell that his father would let him keep Pidge.

Aaron decided to train Pidge to be a carrier pigeon. He tied a little cardboard tube to Pidge's left leg. Inside the tube he put secret messages. Then he had Pidge walk across the living room toward a pile of crumbs. "When your wing is stronger," Aaron told Pidge, "you can fly with messages like a real carrier pigeon."

Aaron told all his friends about Pidge. Soon the whole neighborhood was talking about him. But it was a mistake to let everyone know about Pidge. A gang of older boys lived in the neighborhood. They had their own clubhouse. Aaron wanted to join the gang more than anything else. He wanted to learn their secret words. He wanted to belong. Carl, the gang leader, said Aaron could be a member if he brought Pidge to the clubhouse. Aaron couldn't believe it! He raced home to tell his mother.

---

carrier pigeon, a bird that is trained to carry messages

Language Link

A *genius* is someone who is very, very smart. Circle the father's reason for calling Aaron a genius.

Type of Text: Short Story

Aaron is the main character in this short story. What does he want to train, or teach, Pidge to be? Put a box around your answer. Then write three words that describe Aaron. What kind of person is he?

_____
_____
_____

Check Your Understanding

Carl, the gang leader, tells Aaron that he can be a member if he does something. Underline the sentence that tells what Aaron must do. Why do you think the boys want Aaron to do this?

_____
_____
_____

Reader's Companion   Unit 8

Name _____ Date _____

Check Your Understanding

Underline the sentence that tells how Aaron's mother feels about the gang. Why does she ask Aaron to make something special for Grandma's birthday?

_____
_____
_____

Language Link

The word *present* has more than one meaning. It can mean "something you give." It can also mean "the time happening now." Circle the words that tell what *present* means here.

Type of Text: Short Story

The events in a short story usually happen in time order. However, sometimes events jump back in time. Put a box around the sentence that begins jumping back in time.

Check Your Understanding

Why did the Cossacks attack Grandma's village in Ukraine?

_____
_____
_____
_____

But his mother didn't like the boys. She told Aaron to keep away from them. Then she asked him to make something special for Grandma's birthday. That way he would be too busy to think about the gang.

Aaron wanted to give Grandma something special for her birthday. He thought about what it could be. All at once, he knew. Pidge would be her present! Pidge could carry messages for her. Maybe Pidge could even make her feel better about something that happened a long time ago.

Aaron remembered the story Grandma had told him many times. When she was a little girl in the Ukraine, she had a pet goat. She loved the goat more than anything. Aaron thought she must have loved the goat as much as he loved Pidge.

One day, the people in Grandma's village got some terrible news. They knew the czar hated all the Jewish people. Now, he had ordered his soldiers, the Cossacks, to attack their village. The Cossacks were coming! Grandma's family had to hide quickly in the cellar. Grandma had to leave her goat upstairs. If it made a sound, the soldiers would find their hiding place.

_____

czar, a Russian ruler before 1917

Soon Grandma and her family heard the sound of horses galloping into the village. Then the Cossacks were in their house, breaking furniture and smashing all of their things. Grandma thought the terrible noise would never end, but finally the house was quiet. The family came out of the cellar.

The first thing Grandma saw was her goat. It was on the floor, dead. Grandma was heartbroken. She cried for days for her lost pet. Aaron knew that even now, she was still sad about her goat. But maybe Pidge could somehow replace Grandma's long-lost pet. Wouldn't that be the best gift he could give her?

Aaron was excited that he had thought of just the right present for Grandma. But he hadn't forgotten about wanting to join the gang. A few days later, he met Carl in the street again. "Bring the pigeon to our clubhouse," Carl said. "We've got a new kind of badge for you. A membership badge."

---

badge, a small piece of paper, plastic, or fabric that shows you belong to a special group

---

Reading Strategy: Understand an Author's Purpose

Circle the words that tell what Grandma saw on the floor. Then think about the author's purpose in writing this story. What do you think the author is saying about the way Jewish people were treated in Ukraine when Grandma lived there?

MARK THE TEXT

_____
_____
_____

Type of Text: Short Story

In most short stories, the main character has a problem that he or she must solve. Aaron wants to do two things. Underline the sentences in the third paragraph that tell about these things. Do you think Aaron will have a problem trying to do both things? Explain.

MARK THE TEXT

_____
_____
_____
_____

Reader's Companion   Unit 8

Name _____ Date _____

Check Your Understanding

Put a number next to each thing that Aaron does in the first paragraph. Why is Aaron in such a hurry?

MARK THE TEXT

_____
_____
_____

Check Your Understanding

Does Aaron seem like a genius when he gives Pidge to Carl? Why or why not?

_____
_____
_____

Language Link

The word *match* can mean "a game or contest" or "something used to start a fire." Underline the clues that show what *match* means here.

MARK THE TEXT

Aaron raced home to get Pidge. Gently, he removed the strips of cloth and the sticks. Pidge's wing seemed to be completely healed. With Pidge in his arms, Aaron ran to the clubhouse. Carl came out. "Give me the bird," he said.

"Be careful," Aaron warned. "I just took the bandages off."

"Oh sure, don't worry," said Carl. Then he turned to one of the other club members. "Give Aaron his special badge," Carl said. "And light the fire."

"What fire?" Aaron asked.

"Hey!" said Carl. "Don't ask questions. I'm the leader here. Now light the fire, Al."

The boy named Al struck a match. Soon the fire was glowing with a bright yellow-orange flame.

"Get the rope," Carl said. Another boy brought a rope, and Carl tied it around the bird.

"What . . . what are you doing?" shouted Aaron. "You're hurting his wing!"

"Don't worry about his wing," said Carl. "We're going to throw him into the fire, and you're going to pledge an oath to—"

"No!" shouted Aaron.

"Grab him!" Carl said to the other boys.

Aaron acted quickly. He leaped across the fire at Carl and punched him in the face. Carl slid to the floor and dropped Pidge. Aaron grabbed Pidge and raced out of the clubhouse. But before he could get very far, the boys were on top of him. He fell to the ground. Pidge slipped out of his hands. The rope came loose from around the bird's wings, and Pidge flew away.

At that moment Aaron hated the gang more than he had ever hated anyone in his life. He thought of the worst, the most terrible thing he could shout at them. "Cossacks!" he screamed. "You're all Cossacks!" Then he broke away and started running.

When Aaron got home, his parents and Grandma saw his bloody face and torn shirt. "What happened?" they asked. Sobbing, Aaron told them about the gang, the clubhouse, and the fire. He told them how he had planned to give Pidge to Grandma as a gift. He told them how he thought Pidge was the best present he could ever give her.

---

punched, hit with fists
sobbing, crying with short, quick breaths

Check Your Understanding

Underline what Aaron does when he realizes Carl's plans for the pigeon. What happens to Pidge in the end?

_____

Check Your Understanding

Circle the word that Aaron screams at Carl and his gang. Why does he call them that name?

_____
_____
_____

Reading Strategy: Understand an Author's Purpose

What do you think the author is saying about people who behave like Cossacks, Carl and his gang members, or other bullies?

_____
_____
_____

Reader's Companion   Unit 8

Name _____   Date _____

Check Your Understanding

Circle what Grandma does when she hears Aaron's story. Why does this surprise Aaron at first?

MARK THE TEXT

_____
_____
_____

Type of Text: Short Story

Tell how the story ends. Explain what Aaron realizes.

_____
_____
_____
_____
_____

Reading Strategy: Understand an Author's Purpose

What do you think is the author's purpose, or reason, for ending the story the way he does? What might the author be saying about how to treat others?

_____
_____
_____
_____
_____

Aaron's grandmother looked lovingly at her grandson. Then she kissed him and thanked him for his present. Aaron didn't understand. What was she talking about? Pidge was gone. Aaron didn't have any present for Grandma at all.

Later that night, before he fell asleep, Aaron thought about Pidge. He knew Grandma would have loved Pidge. She would have loved talking to him and taking care of him. But then Aaron realized something else. Grandma would have loved Pidge so much that she would have wanted Pidge to be free. She would have let Pidge go.

And then Aaron knew what Grandma meant when she thanked him for her present. Pidge's freedom was the best gift she could have had. For her, it was as if her goat had escaped from the Cossacks. It was as if her goat were free. Then Aaron fell asleep with a smile on his face.

> Turn the story into a comic strip. Draw pictures of scenes from the story. Put the characters' words in speech balloons (circles with tails that show who is speaking). Share your comic strip with a partner.

CREDITS

Illustrations: 122 all, 125, 128, 131 Esther Baran; 132, 135–137, 140, 144, 151 Liz Callen; 42–43, 49, 51 Oki Han; 21, 93, 95, 104, 111 Inklink Firenze; 153 left, 155 Tom Leonard; 183, 189 Gail Piazza; 52 middle, 54–56 Tony Smith; 4, 8–10, 34, 36–38, 52 top, 53 left, 53, 57, 149, 156, 160, 162–163, 171, 173, 181, 190 bottom, Arvis Stewart.

Photos: 6, 82 left & right, 158, 170 right, Steven Oliver/Dorling Kindersley; 12 Kooyman/Animals Animals; 13, 15 right, 17, 18, 20 all, 30, 62 middle, 78 bottom, 89, 113 left, 172 Getty Images; 14 David Young-Wolff/Photo Edit; 15 left, 22 top & bottom, 23 all, 32 top & bottom, 33 right, 51 top, 63, 72 bottom, 73 middle, 90, 98 all, 105 left, 117, 142 left & right, 145, 151, 152 left, 153 right, 169, 170 left, 177, 190 all, Dorling Kindersley; 16 US Geological Survey; 22 middle, CORBIS; 28, 31, 78 top, Prentice Hall School Division; 32 middle, Firefly Productions/CORBIS; 33 left, Robert Holmes/CORBIS; 33 middle, Superstock; 35 Wolfgang Kaehler/CORBIS; 38 John Van Hasselt/CORBIS Sygma; 39 Keren Su/Getty Images; 52 bottom, 71 bottom, Peter Menzel/Stock Boston; 53 middle, Jose Miralles/SI International; 53 right, Araldo de Luca/CORBIS; 62 left & right, AP/Wide World Photos; 65 Zephyr/Science Photo Library/Photo Researchers; 71 top, Vanni Archive/CORBIS; 72 top, Michael J. Tarkanian/MIT; 73 left, 75 bottom, INAH; 73 right, Yale University Art Gallery/ Stephen Carlton Clark, B.A. 1903, Fund; 73 right, Justin Kerr; 75 top, Neil Rabinowitz/CORBIS; 91 top, Gianni Dagli Orti/CORBIS; 86, 91 bottom, 164, 175, 192 top, Bettmann/CORBIS; 105 right, Ronnie Kaufman/CORBIS; 109 Pat Miller/Stockphoto; 111 Rob Lewine/CORBIS; 113 middle, Ann Jones/Getty Images; 113 right, The Bridgeman Art Library; 116 British Museum; 131 CORBIS/Bettmann; 132 left, James R. Fisher/Photo Researchers; 132 right, Gallo Images/CORBIS; 133 Wolfgang Kaehler/CORBIS; 152 right, Robert A. Tyrell Photography; 153 middle, Joel Greenstein/Omni Photo Communications; 157, 171 Oxford Scientific Films/Animals, Animals; 162 Benvie/Animals Animals; 165 Phil Schermeister/CORBIS; 176, 179, 192 bottom, Smithsonian Institution.

ACKNOWLEDGMENTS

HarperCollins Publishers, Inc. "Aaron's Gift," adapted from "Aaron's Gift" by Myron Levoy from *The Witch of Fourth Street and Other Stories*, text copyright © 1972 by Myron Levoy. Published by Harper & Row, New York.